People Pleasing

Rediscover the Authentic Version of Yourself

(How to Avoid People Pleasing and Achieve General Wellbeing)

James Noriega

Published By **Jackson Denver**

James Noriega

All Rights Reserved

People Pleasing: Rediscover the Authentic Version of Yourself (How to Avoid People Pleasing and Achieve General Wellbeing)

ISBN 978-1-77485-969-8

No part of this guidebook shall be reproduced in any form without permission in writing from the publisher except in the case of brief quotations embodied in critical articles or reviews.

Legal & Disclaimer

The information contained in this ebook is not designed to replace or take the place of any form of medicine or professional medical advice. The information in this ebook has been provided for educational & entertainment purposes only.

The information contained in this book has been compiled from sources deemed reliable, and it is accurate to the best of the Author's knowledge; however, the Author cannot guarantee its accuracy and validity and cannot be held liable for any errors or omissions. Changes are periodically made to this book. You must consult your doctor or get professional medical advice before using any of the suggested remedies, techniques, or information in this book.

Upon using the information contained in this book, you agree to hold harmless the Author from and against any damages, costs, and expenses, including any legal fees potentially resulting from the application of any of the information provided by this guide. This disclaimer applies to any damages or injury caused by the use and application, whether directly or indirectly, of any advice or information presented, whether for breach of contract, tort, negligence, personal injury, criminal intent, or under any other cause of action.

You agree to accept all risks of using the information presented inside this book. You need to consult a professional medical practitioner in order to ensure you are both able and healthy enough to participate in this program.

Table Of Contents

Chapter 1: All About People Pleasing 1

Chapter 2: How People Pleasing Rises 8

Chapter 3: Negative Effects Opple Pleasing 15

Chapter 4: How To Overcome Peoples Pleasing 21

Chapter 5: People-Pleasing At A Cost ... 136

Chapter 6: Boundaries, How To Define, Communicate, And Maintain Them 147

Chapter 7: Ask What You Want 157

Chapter 8: Quit Chasing Approval 166

Chapter 9: Watch Your Language Choice 175

Chapter 1: All About People Pleasing

There are many different ways to define people pleasing. The first step is to understand the individual's characteristics. Fear of being rejected, afraid to say "no" to requests, too much emphasis on other people's needs while neglecting theirs, focus on their own feelings, seek approval from others, and give more to their partners than they receive in their relationships. People pleasers think they're less valuable than others. They may try to hide these feelings from anyone they meet. This makes them appear like a doormat. They often feel that they should be treated as such. People pleasers are able to use deception, lies and dishonesty in order to keep other people from knowing what they really feel and what their inner thoughts are.

People pleasers aim to keep people from feeling sorry for themselves. They will do any thing to help them achieve this goal.

Individuals with this problem of pleasing people will often tell more lies throughout their lives than others who suffer from mental illness. People pleasers have an emotional basis and are motivated to please others. They strive to be kind and perfect so they can appear nice and pleasing to others.

People pleasers fear making mistakes, and they are afraid of being disqualified. They find it difficult to focus on their own needs and feelings and reduce their anxiety. To many people pleasing can cause you to lose your sense of self, and make it difficult to see the real you. To please others means that you will lose some of your own self and may make unfulfillable promises.

Some people find pleasing others so addictive that it becomes a way of life. It may be gratifying to be appreciated by others and feel great, but negative thinking can make you very unhappy. People pleasing can rob you of your true identity, and it will destroy any boundaries.

Realistic and realistic thinking is key to achieving your goals. You must also learn to say no, prioritize and prioritise what is important. Be a good friend to yourself and not depend on others. Social networking can make the pleasant condition even worse. The comments and likes of others will impact your self-esteem as well as how other people view you. Your need for approval will limit your freedom to express oneself. Your need to be liked or noticed by others will make you nervous and cause you to refuse new opportunities.

You will be a people pleaser and your whole life will revolve around helping others. This attitude will gradually start to affect your health and cause a feeling of resentment. Anger will be held back by your desire to help others. If it isn't expressed, it can turn into passive aggression. The urge to make other people happy will lead you to losing yourself. There is no reason not to conquer the condition.

Your self-esteem and confidence are influenced by how you feel about yourself. External approval is not necessary to feel worthy or respected. Although it's fine to be happy or help other people, it can become a problem when it becomes a way of life and you begin to like people pleasing. Be kind to yourself, and don't accept guilt. You must be clear about your boundaries. Don't waste time with people who are only trying to get you.

To be a people pleaser at work, you will need to help your colleagues whenever they need help. This makes it difficult to work late or go home for extra work. Instead of accepting every request, it is better to step back and evaluate your ability to fulfill the project's requirements and whether you have enough time. There are always alternative options if the project is not possible.

First, strengthen your foundation in order to be strong enough to make hard decisions and follow the path that is best for you. It is important to practice not seeking approval for decisions or for those you choose. It is important to be truthful and honest with yourself whenever you commit to new tasks. This might seem difficult to many people, but you can overcome it by learning to say no to certain requests.

If you're a people pleaser, you need to be aware of the signs. These signs often indicate the point at which you go from being generous and kind to being a people pleaser. These signs could indicate that you are a people pleaser.

* You don't have time to take care of yourself.

* Don't voice your concerns to anyone else.

* You must always back down whenever an argument occurs.

* You tend to other people's needs and feelings without thinking about your own.

* You will often say yes when asked.

Because you always do favors to them, many of your closest friends are also close to you. This means that people take advantage of your situation, and they only use you to get their desired results.

* Other people benefit from your relationship. Most of your relationships will be one-sided.

If you have pleasing people signs, you will try to be like others. You may also agree with them in order to fit in. Even though you might not be aware that you do this, there is something inside you that wants others to like you. Your partner might get upset if you don't pay enough attention if you are in relationships. This can make it difficult to understand what your partner wants. Only one thought comes to your mind: How are you going to please him/her? People pleasing happens without you even realizing it. If you have the ability to be liked, you will have difficulty expressing your opinions and feelings. Other people's feelings, needs, and concerns will be all that you care about.

It can be difficult to make everyone happy or meet their needs. However, it is possible. You have complete control over yourself and should make the right decisions. It is important to be your top priority. This will help you perform better in relationships with friends, family, or other people. You don't have to be a winner and you can have different kinds of relationships. Know that you're not an option.

Chapter 2: How People Pleasing Rises

There are many factors that can make someone happy. The main reasons are loneliness and low self esteem. If you don't do a favor, some people may not be interested in being close to you. A fear of being rejected, disapproved and alone might lead you to agree to do what they want. A lack of fulfillment from your parents is one reason people like you. Studies have shown that overactivity (which can impact your social behavior as well as your desires, and also reduces your desire for them), empathy, and being very sensitive are other factors that contribute to people pleasing.

It is believed that children who please their parents were more likely to feel loved if they follow the rules and fulfill their parents' desires. These children would do anything that was against their parent's will and their parents would usually react by withholding their support, love, understanding and encouragement. This makes them feel disapproved, abandoned and rejected. People pleasing habits are developed to maintain closeness and relationship with parents who may not be available at all times for their children.

If a parent is not able to give it, a child can learn people pleasing behavior. People pleaser parents tend to be focused only on their own problems, and not consider the feelings or thoughts of their children. People pleaser children can often be seen as adults and become more attentive to their parents' needs. People pleaser parents can be happy, loving, affectionate and affectionate but become anxious, distant, and absent. This can cause the child to become very confused, anxious and preoccupied. The child who pleases people will eventually learn that his/her parents can be unreliable, but he/she cannot stop relying on them.

A person pleasing child will learn to be proud of their parents, neglect their own needs and focus on people pleasing skills. People pleasing children often don't know the best ways to keep and secure love and connection. This leads to perfectionists who are high-achieving and highly motivated. He/she does not want to know who they are or what they want to do, but is more interested only in what others think he/she should be.

Our parents would often congratulate and praise us for our accomplishments as children, whether it was in exams or other activities. But if they weren't happy with us or didn't like us, they often gave us negative attention. This forced us to change our behavior to ensure that we continue to receive the support and love. It made it difficult for us express our emotions and sometimes we forgot about our wants and needs. People who are happy often come from homes in which the child's needs, feelings, and opinions are not valued, respected, valued, appreciated, or considered important. They were expected as children to look out for the needs and desires of other people.

People pleasers are generally generous, open-minded, and warm. This doesn't mean that they don't have problems. Others actually benefit from the choices made and are benefited by the people they please. People pleasers often feel depressed and have difficulty with loneliness. Here are some ways people can be pleasing.

1) Sexual stereotypes. Many cultures put more emphasis on women getting married and having kids than on building a career. They don't learn to appreciate their talents or how to build their own lives. No one value the good work they do. They are less self-confident and more vulnerable than boys. Boys, however, are considered to be more competent and skilled. They are taught how they can fix any situation. Boys are taught things that aren't important to girls. Parents usually want to decide where

their children will work, which college to attend and what courses to take. Although children are capable of doing other things, and they may even want to do it, their parents will often tell them what they should do.

2) Being nice: Some people like to be liked by others and be nice. However, you may not realize that others might try to take advantage of you and pretend they like what you do. If you keep being nice and doing the things that other people want, you'll eventually become a people-pleaser and won't be able to set limits on how much money you give. To avoid this, be kind to others as well as yourself.

3) Unhappy childhood. Children can become people pleasers in homes that are not loving or physically abusive. To feel loved and accepted by their parents, such children might start to please them. If this isn't addressed, it can lead to a lifetime of bad behavior. Happiness can lead to pleasing

people if you grow up in a happy home where you are both able and willing to share the love and support of others. When one is raised in a loving home, it can be hard to accept the love and support of others.

Fear of being left alone: Some people who like to please aren't content to be on their own and will pay to have others do things for them. Sometimes you might invite your friends and wish to make them feel at home by making them feel welcome and providing all they need. It is important to ask them if they would be willing to do the exact same thing for you. Or if they just want you to give them what they need. If you fear being left alone, then you will be the one calling your friends and asking them for favors.

5) Low selfesteem: Feeling worthless makes it easier for others to profit from your feelings. Focusing on your shortcomings or childhood experiences creates a tendency towards seeking acceptance, respect,

approval and approval from others and ignoring your own needs.

6) Be uncomfortable with your body. Body image is an important tool for self empowerment. Many people, especially women, believe that if you aren't thin, you are fat. Being short or tall can make it uncomfortable to be around others. Insecure people often feel that they cannot be accepted because they don't have the right to. All of us want to be perfect, and we all strive for the best body. However, you should not let your body define you and try to please others in order that you are accepted. You have to be confident in your abilities and accept who you are.

Chapter 3: Negative Effects Opple Pleasing

People pleasing may not seem like a good thing at first. But, you will be giving generously, helping others, as well as being more aware of the feelings, needs, and desires around you. All of this is a good thing, especially if it's about pleasing those you love. It can be very rewarding to devote most of your resources, energy, and time to the people who are important in your life. This is a pleasant and admirable trait that can be admired by many people. You will gain many friends who will respect you and, as a result, increase your confidence and popularity.

You will run into problems when you meet people who want nothing more than to profit from you. Their main goal is to destroy your wealth. People pleasing can often be seen as a necessity, obligation or compulsion. It is important to keep your mouth shut if you find yourself pleasing others too much. An addiction to excessive gratification can lead you to become a slave to your needs and desires, and eventually it can lead you losing respect for the people you really want. If you're a people pleaser and spend most of your time making others happy or attending to their needs, you're more likely not to take care of your own feelings and needs. You will also lose your money if this is something you do.

People pleasing is a way to make others like and respect you. They are often seen as pushovers or doormats because they are so generous. People around them will see them negatively because they are too eager and dependent on them to be trusted. They hide their frustrations and anger, so others won't be able to consider their views and feelings. People who are not happy can have trouble achieving what they want in life, work, or relationships. Low self-esteem, self-neglect or self-neglect are some of the most common outcomes of people pleasing.

They also tend to feel guilty about being in a bad relationship.

It's not healthy to suppress your desires, needs and views. You will be constantly hiding your angers, sadnesses, or frustrations. It will hinder your ability to handle your emotions effectively and healthy. While it is important to assist others who are living in accordance with your principles, values, and integrity, you must adapt to their needs. If you want to live a happy, healthy and fulfilled life, it is important to learn how to say 'NO' to others and to take control of your situation. These are the most common negative consequences of people pleasing.

1) Give up your most important possessions: When you are a people pleaser, you may give up certain things you value in order to help others. This will make it difficult to attain general wellbeing. This could be when a coworker asks for time off from you at work. This could be when you have

something planned for your family and you decide that you will not go.

2) Self-neglect. People who want to please others are more likely to ignore their own needs. They spend their time taking care others rather than managing their stress, planning their meals and exercising to take care of their family. This can lead them to numerous health issues. That's why it is important to begin thinking about you and how you want life to be.

3) Not liking being around their families or engaging in activities: People pleasers will find it hard to enjoy time with family members as they will want to please everyone else. Their family will not be able to enjoy them as they will be thinking about how they can help others.

4) Resentment. Over time, people who do not want to be irritated by others will become more angry with those close to them. Passive aggression will result from

their inability to express anger. Resentment is a common cause of breakups in relationships. You need to be open about your feelings. You must always communicate your feelings, even if it causes others to be upset.

5) Depression, stress, and anxiety: Chronic stress can lead depression and other negative behaviors. This cycle could become a vicious circle if you spend too much time helping others and neglect your own needs. It can be difficult for people to get out from this cycle.

6) Exhaustion or fatigue: People pleasing is a recipe for exhaustion and fatigue. They are always too generous and will make you feel exhausted.

7) Lacking intimacy: People who want to please don't have the ability to build a bond with their family. They are too fixated on other people's needs and feelings.

8) Other negative effects include loneliness, regrets, ambiguous expectations, victimization, victimization and regret.

Chapter 4: How To Overcome Peoples Pleasing

It's great and amazing to know that you have an impact on the lives of others and make them happy. There is a distinction between people pleasing and being kind. People pleasing is a condition you don't realize you have. You'll find yourself putting the needs and desires of others before yours, often without realizing it. This condition could make you a high achiever who isn't afraid to please others. As we have already mentioned, this trait can start in childhood. It makes it possible for children to be people-pleasers as adults. This condition forces one to let go of all his/her feelings, needs, and desires and instead focuses on what other people want. Once you are a people pleaser, there's no turning back. Most of all you will seek approval and acceptance from others.

Excessive flattery of other people can be dangerous and can result in a reduction in self-worth. You may also lose your sense of who and what you are. It is hard to say no, especially if you are a people pleaser. This causes a lot problems with setting and maintaining proper boundaries. Not taking care of your own needs and trying to please everyone else will cause you to feel stressed and fatigued. People pleasers might find it difficult to accept that others are different from them. This can affect their behavior and make them question who they really are. To manage this issue, you need to recognize that you are not helpless and vulnerable. There are many skills you can use to maintain your boundaries.

People pleasing makes it feel like you are a victim to your circumstances. It could be that you spend your weekends working for other people. People pleasers struggle when it comes time to make decisions. They are too concerned about what others think about them, and not considering the potential outcome. If you allow others to make your life, and you give them the right to use you when they want to, then you'll run into problems. Living a life in which we often please others is an assumption. It's up you to decide what your opinion is worth. Stop putting other peoples' opinions first.

You may find it difficult to be yourself again and to put your own feelings and needs first. It's time for you to stop living the life that others want and start living the life that you always dreamed of. You can stop looking at other people's opinions and focus on what you really need. Therefore, it is best to stop focusing on the negative aspects of others and instead focus on your own needs. This will make it easier for you improve your own life. This chapter provides effective steps to help overcome people pleasing, and get a happy, healthy and fulfilling life. Here are some methods to defeat people pleasing.

Learn How to Say "NO"

You can't please everyone. But, you need to make sure your health, mental well-being and happiness are your top priorities. If you continue to do favors for others, you will spend too much time worrying about them and less on your life. You need to be able to say no when someone asks for favors. Because you may be afraid of being rejected, hated, and abandoned, it might be difficult for you to say "No" when others ask. Saying no to some things will allow you to stand up for your dignity and personality by not following every instruction.

If you are asked by a friend to join them at a party but don't like the company, then tell them the truth politely. It's okay to say no to all requests, but it is important that you start small. Find something small that you can decline and communicate this confidently and politely. People who take offense if you say no are not worth pleasing. Friends who do this rarely take offense.

Do Something You Enjoy

There are certain things that you would like to do, but fear others might not like. It's okay to not think about what others think, but just do them because they are fun and you truly want them. You can take a vacation, have a change of look, go to a movie or dye your hair. No matter what you do, you should do it because it is something that you enjoy doing and you don't have to worry about what others think. Do not accept what other people tell you. Be your own boss and do it your way.

No matter what opinions others may have, there are certain things that you should do for your own good. You shouldn't let others' opinions dictate your life. They should, however, only have their opinion. This does not mean you should ignore others, but it does suggest that you listen. However when it comes to decision-making, you should always make your own decisions. In order to make it win-win situations, you need to maintain a balance.

Analyze and Identify Your Fears

If you are people pleaser you may have deep-seated fears that are the cause of your belief in other people's worthiness. You can overcome this tendency by looking at your own thoughts and finding out what fears are causing you to be people pleaser. Some believe that people won't approve if you don't agree with everything they say. You must stop believing that you will lose your job or be abandoned. It is true that only those people should matter in you life who are open to you and accept you as you truly are.

Be True to You

You can learn to say "no" to friends who are going to be watching a movie. This does not necessarily mean that you will see the movie you prefer, but people who enjoy the same movie might prefer it. Although it is a good idea to express your opinions and not make demands, you will remind others of your preferences. Other people can help you with something, and it will make them realize that they aren't able to read your mind. If you don't feel like you can express your feelings, needs or desires and you keep doing too much to help others, then it may be because they are not doing enough for you. It's unfair to allow other people to exploit you. You need to be able to speak up and make your own decisions.

Examine Your Limits

You can compare your boundaries to the ones you usually set for other people and determine how much you're willing or unable to let others take advantage of your vulnerability. Knowing what you are able to accept and reject will allow you to assess what should and shouldn't be done. It's more about setting priorities and understanding what is important to you. Don't let things get outof control, or allow others to make you feel worthless. Be true to yourself, and be realistic about your abilities to help others. But don't let it get out of control.

Are You a people pleaser

People pleasers can be very popular and well-liked. The sweet, laid back personality of people pleasers has its flaws.

Research suggests that narcissists are more likely to be toxic than those who associate with toxic people. Statistics indicate that friends of toxic types have something in common.

Charles Figley of the American Psychological Association is the spokesperson. Toxic friends are one way you can pay for it.

It doesn't matter if you can see it, but you are responsible for this relationship. You may have allowed your friend or family member to treat you poorly or make you feel bad. This could be because you want them or because they don't like confrontation.

Boundaries, People

People pleasers don't always know how to set boundaries. You need to take control of your friendships and let others know what is unacceptable. An anonymous reader told me about a friend who was always the "one-up" person when she spoke of her accomplishments or problems.

It happens all the times. Jessica and I were talking about a promotion we received at work the other night. Jessica said that she had heard of my potential promotion. "Then, she continued to tell me how much my promotion would be superior to hers," says anonymous reader. "I also told her about the problem I was having in my marriage, but you should know that her issue with her boyfriend was far worse."

In this case, the reader might try to establish boundaries by explaining her concerns, and asking her friend to stop "one-upmanship."

Talk It Out

Talk to someone trusted and non-toxic about your concerns. It is often easier to identify the problem when you're outside looking in. This means, it can be easy to see the solution.

It is a good idea not to try and find objective counsellors. Employing the skills and knowledge of a trained therapist will allow you to get the objectiveness that you require. You may also learn new coping methods or find answers.

You might also consider writing a journal or a blog about your issue. Sometimes, simply putting our thoughts into words will help us to solve our problems.

If All Other Measures Fail

If you have tried setting boundaries with your toxic friend and trying to discuss the problem, but failed to reach an agreement, it might be time for you to limit contact or end the friendship. This decision is not easy and shouldn't come lightly. But, when it comes down it, your mental health and sanity are more important than any toxic friendship. If you take care to yourself, you will be able to take care and help others. This is a piece of wisdom that people who want to please often overlook.

Kate Kotler is a BitchBuzz writer and offers these guidelines for getting rid of toxic friends.

There are many ways to communicate with someone: phone, email, or just quit talking. In person is the best method. Invite the person to coffee and lunch. Think about why you don't want them in this part of your life and find non-judgmental ways to communicate it. Kotler says to use "I Statements" which is a way of asserting your opinion without being defensive. "Let the friend understand how your behavior affects you. Bob: I feel upset when they ask me for my advice. Bob: Then tell me that you don't know what you are talking about. Be assertive and clear. You should let the person know that you care about them, but don't feel you have to continue a friendship. Give the person time to respond. They may not realize how they behave, or the thought of losing a friend might encourage them to reflect on their own actions. Stop the conversation if it turns negative.

If you've read my work over time, then you'll know that I have written a lot about narcissism. I began this writing to help me heal, but I soon realized that my readers were equally as interested in this topic.

I am a published author on the subject. It's Not Meant to Hurt: How To Overcome Narcissism and Toxic Love in Relationships. Queenbeeing subscribers get a significant discount on the book at the bottom of this post - if you're curious.

Understanding how a Narcissist works will help you live with or work with one. Understanding the behavior of a narcissist can help you accept it. Accepting the behavior of the narcissist and not taking it personally is possible. You can then emotionally distance from him or her. It is possible to either accept the behavior of the narcissist and gain the strength for you to leave. Alexander Burgemeester, The Narcissistic Living.

Although it is easy to mislead a narcissist into thinking that they are starting a relationship, most narcissistic relationships start just like any other. They go through the normal phases of initial attraction and infatuation before eventually falling in love.

There is no one type of narcissist.

There is no "ideal" or "standard" mate/friend/spouse of a narcissist. However, there are similarities to the relationships. One example is the "honeymoon period" where everything seems perfect and almost too good for being true.

The experience of living with a narcissist in a loving relationship can be thrilling and exciting, as well as soul-suckingly difficult and traumatic. It's usually one or the other depending on when it happens. It can be likened to an emotional rollercoaster.

A narcissist is unable to exist without someone to love him, give his will, be available at any hour and willing to make fun of himself. It is called narcissistic Supply.

What attracts a person to this type of relationship and what keeps them there?

People pleasers have common characteristics with the Partners of Narcissists.

Ross Rosenberg writes, "The dysfunctional codependency dance" has two partners. The pleaser/fixer (codependent), and taker/controller(narcissist/addict) are the opposites. "Codependents, who are giving and sacrificing their time and are consumed by the desires and needs of others, do not know how emotional disconnect or to avoid romantic relationships with narcissistic individuals -- people who are selfish, self-centered. controlling and harmful to them. Codependents find themselves in a "dance floor," attracted by partners who are an ideal counter-match to their passive, submissive and acquiescent dance style.

While victims of narcissism can be physically, culturally, and otherwise different, there are certain commonalities that often unite them. Here, I will use "she" as the pronoun. However, there isn't one victim to narcissism. (But, to be fair to men, they make up the majority of the narcissists).

To expect her to stay with you, she must first be insecure. Otherwise, she will quickly abandon you after the first or the second act of narcissism.

She will likely belittle and degrade him often, while glorifying the narcissist.

Because the partner has a tendency towards punishing herself, she becomes the victim. She may even be a bit of a masochist. She might feel like she "deserves" to live a life of torment.

He makes her his scapegoat and puts her needs last.

Sam Vaknin is the author of Malignant Self Love. He says, "It is through self denial that the partner lives." "She rejects her hopes, dreams, aspirations sexual, psychological, material, and other needs. She also denies her preferences, values and choices. She considers her needs to be threatening as they might bring on the wrath the narcissist.

Narcissists may call themselves "people pleasers" or even "diplomats" but often they become so downtrodden in their relationships that they only react to their former selves.

Diane England, PhD explains that being the partner of a paranoid is not a good idea.

Your house and lifestyle are probably included in this category. They care about making a statement to others, not about providing a comfortable environment or restful environment.

The Vampire To Your Fairy: Why Toxic People are Attracted to People-Pleasers

Calm down, I promise you not to do anything superhuman on your sex. You'll be able to bear with me. It's not a metaphor.

To review, a people pleaser is someone who, intentionally or subconsciously, is so concerned about confrontation, making someone unhappy/sad/uncomfortable/angry or otherwise causing stress in their lives that they will often place their own wants and even needs on hold in order to keep everyone else happy.

The True Blood Connection

I enjoy using some characters from HBO's True Blood to illustrate my entire theory about people-pleasers, and toxic people who are attracted towards them. The "light" fairy is portrayed while the "dark" vampires are.

Sookie, the main protagonist, is a fairy that can hear thoughts from all other beings, including humans and fairies.

When she meets her first vampiric, she falls in love. And why? Because she is unable to hear his thoughts. She cannot hear his thoughts and she is constantly being screamed at by others. Because it's only through HER that he is able to actually walk in sunshine.

People-pleasers can be very empathic, which means that they are able to read and communicate well with others. However, they can become bored if they're so skilled at it. They look for people who are challenging and sometimes find them.

People pleasers? They believe they can fix them. Or maybe we secretly long to be challenged.

So the fairy is to people pleasers what the vampire is to toxic persons. To make matters worse, the toxic person craves a certain level and type of narcissistic supplies (an inexorable stream of people, events, and entertainment to keep him happy), and he is just like the vampire.

Okay, enough metaphors. Let's just get on with it.

Start with Your Head: You are the product of what you think

You have probably heard it all: What you think about is what you get. You attract more of what your attention is focused on. The law of attraction. It may sound easy, but it is possible to forget about it. It may be too simple. People often discount the whole idea because it's so simple.

But, the idea is that one can focus on something, believe something, want it to happen. If you are conscious of what you think, you can have a positive effect on the people and things in your life.

This can also happen subconsciously. It happened to me, for example, when I was taking maternity leave after having my 2nd child. This fact was important to me and I worked hard to focus on it.

Sure, I went back work. I thought every day about being able work remotely. I felt jealous of friends who were capable (which was wrong, as it would have made things much easier). I read every book I could find on working from home. I also discussed the topic with my husband. It was something that I shared with all my family members, friends, and everyone else. I wanted it.

Even though I had just received information about a future promotion the previous day, my boss called me and fired us.

I did not understand why. I was horribly upset and infuriated, but as I drove away, I realized I was feeling lighter than ever before. I phoned my husband to let him know.

We made the decision to move in together and work remotely for a time. I've always been a writer/editor, even though it wasn't my job. Therefore, the transition was easy and motivated.

And here I am, years later. I work from home and follow my passions. This is something I never expected to do, and even less loved, but I am doing it. This was an incredible opportunity and I am grateful.

Gratitude and Abundance are the foundation of connection

The first step to all this is gratitude. Reminding yourself to be grateful is a great way to start.

Shortly after the book had been published, a close friend gifted me a copy Rhonda Byrne's "The Secret". This is yet more example of the concept coming to prominence in my life. It is something I have to believe.

I'm learning to live again. And learning to change my mindset. Changes in my mind are making positive improvements in my life. It's amazing but it is something that works.

I could list many examples of how this concept affected my life.

As I start this new phase of my life, I am focusing now upon the power that is thought. I am making an effort to be conscious of my thoughts and to not think, say, or do anything that would negatively impact my life or the world around it.

Although I'm not a saint, there are times when I allow the everyday to overwhelm me.

Instead of dwelling on negative things and letting it ruin my day (like the cranky husband who wakes up in the morning). I look at the positives and try to move on. (I am grateful my husband works every day to help our family financially so I can take care them in other ways...)

It works. This is only the beginning. Take this journey with me to self discovery, self empowerment. Remember this: YOU are what YOU THINK.

Live it, Learn it, Love It. It's real.

Haters Gonna Hate: Dealing w/ Jealous People

I hope that you're seated, because I'm about blown your mind. Here's something you might not have known: Haters really are gonna hate. This is a fact that has been proven true by a scientific study.

The Journal of Personality and Social Psychology published it in 2014. Katy

Waldman of Stuff.co.nz says that the study supports the Hip-Hop and Internet truism "You just can't beat some people."

Waldman writes, "In their paper Attitudes Ohne Objects psychologists Justin Hepler & Dolores Albarracin demonstrate that people with negative views tend to be more inclined to react negatively when presented with new stimuli." "The pair asked 200 men to reflect on how they feel about different subjects like camping, Japanese architecture, crossword puzzles, and taxidermy.

Researchers were particularly attentive to those who rated many unrelated prompts very harshly.

Thirty days later researchers asked the group for a second weigh-in to verify that the haters weren't just bad moods from the first encounter.

Waldman continues:

"After marking hateful haters in scarlet H, the researchers gave information to participants about a new product, the 'Monahan LPI800 compact 2/3-Cubic Feet 700-Watt Microwave Oven."

Although the microwave did not exist, the participants knew that and they were given three positive as well as three negative reviews.

While those who stated they enjoyed crossword puzzles or taxidermy, also indicated they liked the microwave oven, those who were identified by the hater label also spread the hate during fake consumer surveys. These people were more likely not to be positive about recycling or vaccines.

Do you see my point now?

I am bringing up this study to prove that:

1. You are not the only one who is enraged.

2. Haterade, a term that is frequently used to describe hateful behavior, is popular among those involved.

3. Scientists agree that haterism exists.

You probably read this article because, just like me, it's shocking to learn that there are haters. You shouldn't let that get to you. They might think you are a little too extraordinary for them. These folks might even be called "born losers". Why?

"Haters always win. It's something I believe is true in life. In the end, negative energy always pays. Tom Hiddleston

Before we go any further into this comprehensive guide to dealing haters, let us first define a few key terms.

1. Hater — UrbanDictionary.com defines hatred as "a person who can't be happy for another individual's success." Instead of feeling happy, they point out a flaw within the other person.

Hating, which is the result being a hater of someone, is not jealousy. Haters aren't trying to hate the person they dislike, but to get someone down a notch.

2. UrbanDictionary.com, Haterade. A figurative spirit that represents a mode. It is believed that those who drink it are also consumed by the negativity they share.

Anatomy of a Hater

"The downside of multi-talented people is that they can sometimes be intimidated. Some are jealous. You might get some haters. These are disapproving critics that express (and spread negative opinions about) you. "Hate is more about the haters than about you or your situation. It's likely that they are wishing they had done more. Jealousy should be dismissed immediately.

Of course, she's right.

Don't drink the hateful. It's not very flavorful.

Do you want to know the #1 reason why people hate you most? I don't know what it is about me, but I've had my share insecurity over the years. Some I still actively manage.

However, I have come to realize that being jealous of others is not a good thing. It does the exact opposite. It puts my vibe in a state where it is not needed. When my energy isn't happy? I'm not either.

Do not let me fool, however, as this was not a quick transformation. (See my book Project Blissful for the details.

But, after losing 100 pounds, building my career around my passion, and moving with my family to a new beautiful home, I found joy in sharing these successes with my friends and family. This is why I am so thankful.

I was surprised to see that my family and friends weren't all happy for me. They ask me "How can they afford this?" She also wants to know "Who does she think she's?" "What do your day look like?"

I lost a couple of girlfriends, along with my 100-pound body weight. I also lost some more when I moved to a new neighbourhood.

Unrelated relatives called me "greedy" and other things, which I will not mention here. This was after an unprovoked attack on Facebook that I did not understand.

What does that mean?

Why is it that people don't like you when success comes your way?

THE ONE REASON IS: They are insecure.

Insecurity and a lack in self-confidence are the main reasons people act jealousy and haterlike. Period.

To clarify, let's break it down. First, check out Dr. Lissa Rankin's top tips for dealing with haters. First, you must know: It is okay for you to reach your greatest potential.

10 Tips For Stepping Into Your Greatness

1. Nobody can dim your light but you.

2. The only way to make others feel better is to reduce it. It makes you feel worse.

3. Narcissism is not synonymous with confidence. Narcissists lack confidence and overcompensate in order to compensate.

4. Your greatness attracts more people than it repels when you step into it.

5. The confident are sure they will always land butterside-up. They take greater risks, are less likely to fail, and shine brightest.

6. All you need to do is try your best. Your greatness does not have to be achieved by reaching some impossible goal. Your light will shine when you do your best.

7. Being confident means managing your fear. When your fears outpower your confidence, you dim your light. Your greatest achievement is to face your fears head-on, and choose not to allow them to dictate your decisions.

8. Your strength is found in your vulnerability. You don't have to shout your praises. Sometimes your greatest strength is found in your flaws.

9. It's fine to brag. While your weaknesses may be your strengths, it is also acceptable to proclaim your triumphs. Imagine if everybody gave permission to say "I rocked this today!" What if every conversation started with the question "What's great about your life?" Wouldn't that make life more wonderful?

10. You don't deserve credit for your greatness. In this wisdom is your humility. Our egos can be a barrier to the Divine

shining through us. It's not your intention to dim the Divine light through you.

Read more: It's OK for You to Be Awesome: Step into Your Greatness

They think you don't deserve your success.

They think they do. One of my husband's critics who has a physical job would like to point out that my husband "just sits in front the computer all day."

He does not acknowledge that my husband has a lot of intelligence and is highly skilled. He is an IT Engineer for a biomedical organization.

This man, in my opinion, is extremely insecure in himself. He uses it as a way to lower his self-esteem. By putting down the jealous man, he makes a small improvement in his own self-esteem. This is true even though it may seem sad.

In reality, however, he makes himself look like an enormous jerk who is overindulgent.

My husband made those choices that lead him to his 'cushy desk job', while his friend made the choices that led them to their physically challenging job (in a company that he owns).

They want what they have.

It doesn't matter what it may be, whether it is a car or a baby, a house, or something nice, something in yours is perceived as more valuable than something else in their lives.

It is okay. It doesn't make you feel bad.

They're just assholes.

Sometimes people just act like jerks. Or they might be trolls. It doesn't matter what you call them, some people just hate you for the sake hating.

Many times, they're so passionate about drama that sometimes they'll even go as far as to hate someone else. They post their latest dramas on Facebook or Twitter and all they want to do is moan about their lives.

These are the types of people you wish weren't related to yours because they are often the most difficult.

So, how do you deal the hate?

"Haters don't stop hating. Someone has gotta do it." Chris Brown

Blow them out

Kim Kardashian's strategy might work for someone like you. She just laughs at her critics.

Kardashian is quoted saying that "When there's such a lot of haters and positive things, I really do not care."

If empathy is possible for this person, you can recall a time in your past when you were feeling so insecure and upset. Just ignore the behavior. Keep smiling.

This is easier said than done. Keep reading if that doesn't work. I have more.

Use it as a compliment

Jennifer Lopez, multitalented mama, said that haters didn't bother her. She has a totally different view.

Lopez says, "I joke that you should let the haters motivate your," Lopez adds. Lopez said, "Everybody has someone in their life who makes them feel less than they actually are." It's all about faith and belief in oneself, and you need to really dig into it. This must be yours - nobody can give it to you.

I sort of get what she means. When I lost 100 lbs, I noticed something weird when I visited restaurants and shops where women congregated, particularly when their men were there.

I would often get the "old up, down" look from a few of them. At first I thought that I might be a boog. I eventually realized that it was the same look I used when I felt insecure about my self.

At first, my desire was to cry. In this instance, the hating was more a. compliment than an insult. So I now just smile at the people and secretly express my gratitude.

They can be killed with kindness

I know you think they don't deserve it. It's not easy to be mean when someone is always sweet to your face.

I cannot count the number of haters that I've made friends, or at most polite acquaintances with this way. It's well worth the effort. However, if you cannot kill them with kindness it's best to avoid fueling their jealous fires. Pay attention to the following rule:

It is overrated to retorts or revenge.

Ryan Lochte insists that he doesn't allow the haters to get too close to him. He doesn't even bother responding to them.

"I try not take in negative comments. And when I do, I just let it go. Lochte reminds me that there will always been haters, as long as you're in the public eye."

You don't have to call a hater out or expose their hate to the world. It is tempting. The only thing you would do is to lower yourself to their level. The behavior is more attractive to the rest of the world than it is to you.

Your haters are free to dig their own graves. You are too busy living your life.

Don't apologize

You can give people a little power by apologizing out of habit and to keep them quiet. Let's just keep moving forward. Just keep your head up and don't apologize if you do something that caused you pain or hardship. Remember, people have the power to choose how they feel about their lives. This can and should apply to you. Let's see things as they are and see what happens.

People have sent me extremely rude messages since I posted photos from my home decorating projects on Facebook. Same applies for vacation photos, happy statuses of family members and other.

What's more? My husband and me have worked tirelessly to get here and I am proud of it. We love what we do and won't ever be sorry. We shouldn't judge you.

Make #1 happy first

Here's what you need to know. There is something extraordinary about being happy with your existence. You stop valuing opinions from others more than yours. Haters can't take you down if your love for your life is strong.

Let me ask, is worrying about these people going offer you any sort of benefit? It will only cause more stress. Remember: You create what you think. You should think about what it is you want and not what it isn't.

Do your own inventory

If you feel upset about your hateful friends, it might be time to do a personal inventory. You might need to change something about your life.

Keep being your fabulous self

Bottom line, hater will always hate no matter who you or what your background. But they shouldn't steal your sunshine honey. Your light is too precious to let anyone force you to hide. Be positive and love yourself and continue moving in the right directions. Nobody's opinion is worth losing heart over. Okay? Okay, now let's move on.

How to handle being underestimated

"When someone judges another, they don't define you, but you define you." -Wayne Dyer

Did you ever find yourself in a situation that someone underestimated you in any way? Do you think the offender misjudged how intelligent, strong, or competent you are?

Did you find yourself believing that the person was right, or were you defensive or angry at him/her for being wrong?

Nearly everyone has been the victim of unfair judgments. People judge people based on their looks, their weight, their financial (and parental) status, where they live, what religion they practice, and how successful or unsuccessful they are in their careers.

This is especially true for people who don't know you well, but it can happen in families and friendships.

Even people with high self-esteem can feel frustrated when they're wrongly judged. However, those who feel they're not enough can experience feelings of inadequacy if the insult is thrown their way.

How can you deal with people who misunderstand you or make assumptions about you?

Let it roll off of your back

In certain cases, it's better to just ignore them than deal with them again. It can be upsetting to receive rude comments or remarks from a customer at a clothing retailer. If you really think about it, those people may not be there again once you've left the store.

Remember that you are the one who decides who has power in this scenario, so take it! Don't let someone else ruin your day. Instead, choose happiness. (If it helps, remember that the "best revenge is living well" mantra.

Be Proud of Yourself. Or not.

You have a few options to choose from if the underestimator are people you know. You have the option to speak up or take action if you feel it is important.

Don't try to defend or confront the judge. They won't listen to you if you're underestimating them. And you'll be more upset if they won't even acknowledge the validity of your words. It invites negativity into your lives.

It is essential to get comfortable with who you are and how you see yourself. It's unlikely that you will feel the need or desire to prove yourself if your body is healthy and comfortable.

It Hurts

It can sometimes hurt to be underestimated, especially in professional and personal settings. It doesn't matter whether it hurts you or your pocketbook; it can make it difficult to be happy with yourself and/or the people in your life.

Keep in mind that it's important to not judge or underestimate yourself when this happens. It's extremely unlikely. Everyone has faults. And in most cases, one man's flaws is another man's treasure. Be proud of yourself and realize that you are uniquely YOU. That's all that matters.

While it is easy to feel hurtful when you are unfairly criticized, you will only be harming your self by doing so. It is important to remember that the world you put out will come back to you. So if you feel unfairly treated, you most likely will.

Keep in mind that people who feel the need constantly to judge and disparage others are most likely insecure within themselves. They are probably wrong, and not you.

You are Not Alone

This has happened to almost everyone, I'm sure. Take me as an example. One of my coworkers thought I wasn't smart enough for me to even make coffee.

It did frustrate me, and I must admit it. I knew for certain that I was much more capable and skilled than this person. I wanted to tell her exactly what my thoughts were of her.

A second admission is that I did not have many pleasant thoughts about her after she had blatantly misjudged and dismissed me without asking me who I am and what I could accomplish. (She made an incorrect assumption. Do you know what happens when people ASSUME right?

Despite my strong emotional reaction, I took a step back to evaluate the situation. If I was to do the diarrhea of a mouth thing, it could severely impact my career and that job. So I decided to change my mind. Despite my personal feelings, I managed to keep a professional and friendly relationship. And she finally understood that I knew exactly what I was doing. Even though we were "work friends", they became even closer.

It was for me that making peace and finally being acknowledged for my abilities was a better choice than blowing up and ruining any chance of it happening. So, what's the moral? Remember to think before speaking and not allow the bastids to get you down

Approval? You don't need to have your Stinking Approval (Except yours)

"Our deepest fear not is that we are insufficient. Our deepest fear stems from our belief that we are strong beyond measure. It is our light and not our darkness that scares us most. We ask ourselves "Who am we to be brilliant and beautiful, talented, famous?" In reality, who is it that you don't want to be? You are a Godchild. You are not serving the world by playing small. Shrinking to ensure that others don't feel insecure about you isn't a smart thing. We were meant to be a witness to the glory and goodness of God. It's not only in some people, but in all of them. We unconsciously allow others to see the light in our eyes, and we are able to let it shine in return. When we are free of our fear, our presence automatically liberates other people." Marianne Williamson

Good news: It's possible to get away from the approval of others

Most of us were taught as children that it was possible to make others happy. Most children desire approval from their parents, teachers, friends, and family. We tend to have the same urge into adulthood. While it's natural for us to seek out the approval and support of others, sometimes that might not be the best thing.

A strong and independent person can move freely in the world without being restricted by others' opinions. Think about the people that you value the most. Do they allow others' opinions to influence their decisions? You can also live this way.

These tips can help you live your best life.

Learn to be frank about your thoughts. You might be worried about others' opinions.

* Get involved in smaller issues. You can give specific answers, such as if someone asks you what movie you'd like.

* Speaking up about important matters will become easier as you gain more comfort.

Make time for yourself. Remind yourself every day for a few minutes to appreciate all that you love about yourself. Keep a list of all the good things that you do each day. List your positive characteristics.

* Approval of oneself is a better way to go than approval from others.

Keep in mind that it is impossible to please everyone. There are many people around the globe. You will never be liked no matter what you do. Strangely, people who try to please everyone tend not to be respected. People admire confident people.

There is more gray area than you may think. People who are desperate to be accepted by others believe perfection will make them happy. You won't be considered a saint or condemned for your daily words and actions.

* It's not unusual for the best people to do or say things that others would consider to be bad. Other people realize that no one is perfect. Do you judge people harshly because of minor problems?

Be respectful of others' disapproval and don't encourage them to criticize. People often use disapproval as a means to control others. It is possible to reward someone by using disapproval to make unneeded excuses or to change your mind.

* If you feel another person is being unreasonable, think about confronting them in an amiable, calm manner. You will soon find that the criticizers tendencies to criticize you stop when they don't affect your choices. It is fair to show disapproval given the circumstances. You will find that disapproval works for you once in a while and not against.

Before you do anything, think about whether you are primarily doing it in order to gain approval. Be aware of the things and people in your life that make you feel superior.

* Do something you enjoy each week, even though they may not be a big hit with anyone. It gets easier over time.

Everyone seeks approval from other people at times. Allowing yourself to feel controlled by your thoughts and behavior can make your life less enjoyable and more difficult.

Recognizing approval-seeking thoughts or behavior as they occur is the first step towards changing them. You will find that the disapprovals you avoid have much less impact on your life than you realize. It's not that big of a deal. It's not necessary to have the approval of others. You'll be grateful you did.

How to stop Caring about What Others Think (Without Looking Like A Huge Jerk).

There is an eternal internal struggle that many of us have to deal with every day: do we make our own decisions and create happiness or are we influenced by the opinions and judgments made by others (and society)?

We fear what might happen if others don't accept our will that we find it hard to make our own decisions. What will their opinions be of us? What will their opinions be? Are they going to think that we have all become huge jerks??

Kate's story

Kate, 37-years old, says that her father has always dictated what she does. He forced Kate to go to his school and choose the same career path as him. For her college graduation gift, he bought her a place next to his house and offered her a job with his firm. He also steered her towards a certain man when he felt it was time to get married. He has effectively made every major decision in her life for her, or coerced and manipulated her to do so. She is angry.

Let's see this in context, shall we?

Kate, a 37 years old woman who is capable financially and physically of taking care of her family, feels that her father will leave her if she doesn't do what he tells. Kate admitted that she fears her father won't love Kate if he doesn't tell the truth. However, she knows deep down that she believes she's obligated by him to do the right thing because without him she wouldn't be Alone In the World.

Do you recognize Kate

Kate seems to have a problem similar to many people: she is a people pleaser. She has learned how to be a people pleaser, which she learned early in her childhood.

Earley stated that parents can be very strict and tell children what to do. They will never encourage their kids to make decisions for themselves. "When kids obey, parents give them conditional affection."

Time to make a decision

This is the bottom line: If you want happiness, then you have to look within and discover what you really want. It's up to you to pursue it, no matter how annoying it might be.

It's easier said that done, I know...but it's possible. Living a life designed and approved for you by someone else. Pick your poison, folks.

You can choose to be happy and follow your heart or to do what someone else tells you. Then, deal with the consequences. If you choose happiness and make your own choices, you are my hero.

Have a different perspective

The worst thing that can happen is when you make a decision with someone that you don't agree with. There will be a short period of discomfort before that person accepts your decision. You may find some people who would be willing to cut you out of your life for such an offense. However, those are the people that love and like you only conditionally. ("If I tell you to do what I want, then I'll love it.")

Are you really ready for people who have such control over your life and decisions? Reevaluate the relationship. Is it toxic?

Believe (and do) What You Are Saying

The biggest reason people are comfortable telling your what you should do in your life is because you expect (and accept) them to. It can make it difficult to trust your inner voice.

Be confident when you make unpopular decisions in your personal and professional lives. When someone questions your decision, smile. You can then move on.

You can help the person feel validated by acknowledging and being grateful that they have taken the time to give you their opinion. This will make it easier for them to accept you decision. Keep in mind that you aren't asking for permission. You are stating a fact - this is a choice you have made. End of discussion.

Earl offers a Cue

My Name is Earl is a TV series that I'm sure you have seen. Earl seems like an ex-convict who lives in a motel and shares his bed with his brother. He is unique if you give him a second glance. He observes people and situations around himself, but never judged or dismissed them. He doesn't react negatively; he just observes.

Remember that the law of attraction is that like attracts. This means that if your focus is on disapproving people or situations in others' lives, it will be more likely that they judge or disapprove you. You'll find acceptance in others if you focus on yourself.

Accept your Self

How about accepting other people? If you find yourself secretly criticizing and judging your own choices, it is time to discover why. Is it because of something you feel is wrong? It's time to evaluate your motivations and discover why.

Is it that someone else believes what you do is wrong even though you are happy doing it? If so, it's high time to take control of your life and be the person you want to be. People who love your happiness will be happy for you.

Real Friends: Build, strengthen and identify true relationships

You probably know that friends change, and sometimes it is best to move on with your life. Sometimes your interests shift as you age. Sometimes you must part ways with friends you once considered to be your best friend. At the end, however, it's possible to identify friendships that have a strong foundation.

How can you tell which relationships are "real?"

These truths are what you need to know in order to identify true friendship.

1. Friendship endures disagreements. Everyone you consider a true friend will agree that disagreements are inevitable.

However, this person can also verify that your bond is resilient to disagreements.

* True friends recognize that no matter how many disagreements there may be, the foundation of the friendship will always remain.

* When two people can live peacefully with one another after a disagreement, it is an indication of true friendship.

2. Friends keep it real. The beauty of friendship is that it rarely involves pretense. Friends share their vulnerability with one another. They trust that one another will accept their quirks.

* Your true friends won't worry about how you feel about their behavior or actions. They know that the only person who understands them is you.

It's safe to say that you can trust your friends to not sugar-coat any of their opinions. Expect to get as real an opinion from them as you can!

3. Confidentiality is respected. If the topic of confidentiality arises, you can inform a friend by asking whether confidentiality has been granted. True friends recognize the importance maintaining trust.

It is easier to share your deepest secrets with trusted friends. Friends are just as safe as your secrets if you keep them private.

A true friend knows that you value your privacy and will protect it. They can help you decide when to let go and give you the space you need. And they do so without being offended.

4. All support is unconditional. Friends may share different beliefs or interests. Friends can be supportive even though they may have different views.

* Friends will often give each other advice. Even if the advice you get doesn't match

what you are looking for, you can tell it's genuine.

* You know your true friends when you need someone to turn to in times of trouble. They'll be there when you least expect them to and will always bring lots of hugs.

5. Everyone should be proud of their achievements. It is very unlikely to meet a true friend who doesn't acknowledge your achievements. However, some friends will envy your success. True friends feel just as excited by your victories.

* You will likely find a genuine friend who can help you prepare to interview for a job. Even if the success is their own, they will be content knowing that you stand a good shot of winning.

* Sincere friends take the effort to be kind and congratulate one another. They gift each other gifts, make special gestures, and

take turns cooking for one another. They want to show how much they care.

Do these signs help you to identify a friend? If you have, keep that person close to your heart! It can be difficult for someone to be a friend. Your friendships can bring you great joy.

Your commitment to being a friend to others is as important as it is to yourself. Friendship can work both ways.

Dealing with co-workers who are annoying

What do YOU do when your job is all you love, but one coworker is annoying? This person needs to be your friend at least 8 hours per working day, 5 days a week. You spend more time with this person then you do with some of your friends and family.

Some people love to push our buttons. To make it harder for you to succeed, there are people who will actively hinder your progress. Some people are totally clueless and don't realize what they're doing. This is how you would feel if you worked with someone like them.

Find some great tips on how to deal with irritating coworkers

1. Avoid them. Although it might seem obvious, avoiding someone can help you reduce your interactions with them.

2. It is okay to ignore annoying coworkers. Do not work with an annoying coworker.

3. Try to keep a positive attitude and take the high road. You can let the irritating behaviors go, but you must not be annoyed by them. Your job is to remain focused and get the job done.

4. Find a way you can vent your frustration. It is best to get away from those who are annoying you. You should not take breaks and go to the bathroom where they could be seen. Instead, take a short walk and let them go.

* Power walking is more than just a slow stroll. You can get rid of your frustrations with a quick workout. The endorphins that you release during exercise can make you feel much better.

5. Be more assertive. You can't avoid someone or ignore them. If that doesn't work, then confront them.

* If a coworker is constantly singing or cracking jokes with others, tell them politely that it's distracting. Say that you would appreciate it if your coworker focused on their work.

* If you find a coworker interrupting your work flow, write them a note or send an e-mail to let you know. They should respect your time and only talk to them if they have pressing work-related questions.

6. Talk to your manager. If you try all of these methods and still don't see any improvement, it may be time for your boss to intervene.

Your supervisor might be able to convince them to stop their annoying behavior.

* It is also possible that other people have the same concerns. If coworkers or supervisors have expressed similar concerns, they will not hesitate to address it.

You should remember that an annoying coworker is usually unhappy with their own life. You can either show compassion or avoid someone who is suffering. Do not let their misery interfere with your work.

You can instantly be liked by others without being too nice

Rapport is a relationship that fosters harmony. It's the feeling people feel when they have a good relationship with someone. Establishing trust is crucial in all relationships we have, whether they're with our family members, friends or coworkers.

8 Tips to Make Instantly Popular - How to Create Quickly Relationships

These techniques can help you to establish rapport and instantly make friends with almost anyone.

1. Small talk is important. Choose your topics carefully. Avoid engaging in silly arguments while creating reports.

* Talk about topics that you consider safe, such as a favorite restaurant or a recent vacation.

Avoid politics and religion. These topics can be very emotional and lead to heated discussion.

2. Talk about their favorite subject. If you have difficulty coming up with topics for conversation, ask them questions.

* You can find out their interests and see if they've been to any movies.

3. Show empathy and genuine concern. Try not to look disinterested or tense when you are asking questions. This could be detrimental to your relationships.

* Instead, lean forward, nod your chin occasionally, and let them know you're interested.

4. Everyone appreciates a sense humor. There is no need to be "on" all the time when you are talking to someone. You can share a humorous anecdote or a joke with your partner to help build rapport. Being able to laugh with someone will make them more likeable.

* Be safe and tell a joke about your situation. To be humorous, you should not make critical remarks about others. This could backfire on you and have the exact opposite effect.

5. Listen to the information being shared by others. Are they saying "I see your point", "I

can hear what you are saying", or "I feel the exact same way?"

* It is possible to tell whether someone is visual, auditory, kinesthetic, by listening to what they say. You can use similar language to establish rapport.

6. Don't appear too desperate. Some people tend to be too aggressive when making new friends. Overdoing things and trying to be too hard can cause others to leave rather than building rapport.

7. Give genuine compliments. You can end up putting others down if it is obvious you are trying to slap them or over-praising them.

* While compliments are flattering and appreciated, we appreciate being praised when it's real.

8. Mirror the person that you are speaking to. Mirror the person you're trying establish

a connection with. It's important to not make it too obvious. Copy what they do.

* Let's say someone crosses their legs. Wait a while and then cross your legs the opposite way. If they scratch their nose or rub their ear, wait a moment and then do another.

* Duke University psychologists did a study to prove the effectiveness of this strategy. They had 37 students experiment with a new sports beverage. After they tried the drink, students were asked a series questions. During the questioning the researchers mirrored half the participants.

* Researchers discovered that people who were mirrored reported that they were more likely buy and consume the energy drink they were being questioned about.

Use this technique with subtlety and you will be amazed at its effectiveness. Imitating is the best form flattery.

You can establish rapport quickly, no matter whether you're trying for a new friend or a date.

Self-Soothing - How to get started and what to know

How can you help yourself to be more relaxed? It matters!

Since our infancy, we have learned many methods to reduce negative emotions. How we make our bodies feel better can impact the type of challenges we face. There are positive, neutral, or negative ways to handle stress. Negative treatment of stress can have grave repercussions.

Positive strategies can make life so much easier.

Below are some examples:

1. Food. Eating as a way to alleviate stress or sadness can often lead to obesity, and other health concerns. Eating is a popular way to

feel better. Ask yourself before you eat if you are hungry.

2. Shopping. Avoiding unnecessary purchases can lead to financial difficulties. The temporary pleasures of spending money are very short-lived. Additional financial stress, on top of other problems, isn't going help.

3. Do not use drugs or alcohol. Drugs can make it difficult to get work done and manage life. Your health is also at risk. You may also be subject to financial pressure. For those who are using drugs or alcohol to cope, it is a good idea to seek professional assistance.

4. Sex. Use of sex to soothe can lead you to unwanted pregnancy or other sexually transmitted diseases. Although it is fun and exciting, sex can also be a distraction that can lead to problems in your daily life.

These methods of dealing stress are not effective in addressing the root causes. They can lead to more stress in future. This isn't a complete list. Take a look at your coping skills and see if they are effective.

Examples of neutral strategies

1. Television, reading or cleaning, as well as any other distractions. These distractions are not likely to bring about additional harm, but they do provide a way to get the solution.

They can even provide some benefits. Reading materials such as the one below can help. Not to mention the benefits of a cleaner home. But, the source of stress is still there.

2. Spending time together. This could be beneficial depending on how you spend your time. It is not neutral if it serves only to distract you.

You can use neutral strategies to self soothe, so you won't be adding more challenges. But, you can handle stress in even more effective and efficient ways.

Some examples of positive strategies

1. To focus on solutions. Solution-oriented thinking will help you eliminate your stress. It can help reduce stress levels by getting your mind off the problem and directing it toward finding an answer.

2. Have a conversation about your challenge with someone. You're more likely to get new insights, and you will also be happier. Make a list and brainstorm ways to get rid of the emotional distress.

3. Journaling. You can reduce stress by writing down your thoughts. Not only will you be able to save your thoughts and memories for later reference, but it also gives you the opportunity to record your entire life.

Are you positive about your self-soothing? These methods don't offer instant relief, but they do require you to confront the stressful situation. Good news is that you are dealing with the root cause.

Create a list of five ways you can deal with your sadness, fear, or stress. These options should be more positive than the current strategies. Which strategy is most likely for you? Each person is unique so there's no one answer that will work for everyone.

Everyone has their own primary strategy for managing uncomfortable feelings. What's yours? How can self-soothing be made easier? A positive way to relieve negative emotions is priceless. Your emotional pain can be managed in a way that does not create additional difficulties but confronts the source.

9 Essential Questions That You Must Ask To Help Grow

One argument could be made that living is a way to discover more about yourself. Effective questions are a way to improve your human development. A good question will provide you with a useful answer. Poor questions create limitations.

These questions will enhance your development.

1. What's the most important skill you lack? Everyone has weaknesses and strengths. Our weaknesses can be limiting to our personal growth, and even hindering our success. Being well-rounded is a good thing.

* You might be good at spreadsheets but terrible at meeting new people. Some people are persuasive while others have great creativity.

* What are the things you feel lacking in life? Which skill is most likely to fill that void for you?

2. How can I stop myself from getting in my own way? Have you ever tried to undermine your own efforts and failed? It is possible for success to be feared. In the end, sometimes

gaining something requires you to give up something else. It can be hard to recognize this part of yourself. But the benefits are tremendous.

3. What advice would you give to your 18-year old self if you could travel back in history? You can't see the future, but you may still be making the same mistakes in the past. Now think back to the 18-year-old choices you made. They will help you understand your current situation.

4. What are some of my greatest strengths and weaknesses? Create a list of all your strengths. What are your greatest strengths? How can you use them in your everyday life? Although our weaknesses might keep us from reaching our full potential, our strengths will allow us to rise. Weaknesses act as a boat anchor and strengths work like a motor.

* You can also ask your family and friends for their opinions.

5. What is the most I can control in this life? Your time is wasted if you worry about things outside your control. Be focused on the things that can be changed. Your thoughts, time, effort, and efforts should be directed accordingly

6. What are my values? How would you like to be viewed at the end your life? Is it possible to live your life in a way that supports that vision?

* Think about the person you want and how it might differ from what you currently are.

7. What would you choose to do if you could achieve one great thing in your life? There are likely many options available for you in your life. It can be hard to decide.

* Think about what accomplishment would be the most meaningful to you. You can then make a list if you are realistic about the steps required to achieve that goal.

8. What is the most restrictive thing I've ever put on myself? It could be that you don't have the intelligence or social skills to succeed in college, or to find the right person to marry. 99.999% chances are you haven't worked hard enough in order to know your limits.

* How can this be overcome?

9. Who or what is to blame? You can be sure that your parents made mistakes. Perhaps your boss can be a jerk.

* You are responsible for addressing your challenges regardless of their source. This knowledge is great because it means that you no longer have to rely upon others to make progress.

The questions are a great tool. Questions can provide greater insight and clarity. You can use the power to ask questions to keep you on your path of self-growth.

Blush, Go Ahead! Why and How to Accept Compliments

Sometimes compliments can make us feel good about ourselves, but sometimes they can make us squirm. These helpful tips will help you to feel more comfortable in the spotlight. You will soon find yourself surrounded by praise and giving kind words to others.

How giving more compliments helps

You can learn to accept compliments by being kind and giving them. It's because people will respond positively to your praise. Also, you will get more compliments and create a happier environment.

Here are 12 Secrets for Accepting Compliments Even if You Feel Blush

These strategies will allow you to praise your employees like a pro.

1. Be genuine. Most important is authenticity. Seek out the positive qualities

in others you admire and desire to acknowledge. People will generally appreciate your sincerity, especially if your intentions are pure and honest.

2. Pick something. It is nice to let someone know that they are valued employees and that their home is beautiful. It's even better if you can pinpoint what you like most about them. Remark on how they cut their travel expenses by three times or how skillfully the sponge-painted their bathroom walls.

3. Use your imagination. Most yoga instructors know that she's flexible. You might notice her smiling more if she makes people feel at home.

4. Act quickly. Your compliments may make more impact if they are delivered promptly. Let your grandmother know how much the sweater means to you. This will help you to learn how to speak up when doubts start to set in.

5. Gush a little. Don't be afraid to get a little crazy. Many cooks will gladly invite the guest back to dinner if they feel that your eggplant Parmesan reminds them of Parma.

6. Write it down. It's easier to praise when it is written down. Send emails and send greeting cards.

7. Go public. Gather a larger audience if necessary. You can thank your staff accountant for simplifying forms regarding travel expenses and timesheets by holding a staff meeting. The next time you meet up for dinner, mention your spouse's promotion.

8. Spread good news. You can also use compliments received from others. Your best friend is likely to be delighted if your children pass on flattering remarks about her ghost stories.

Accepting Compliments Graciously

These proven methods will prove to be a great way to get complimented next time you are told you are fabulous.

1. You need to assess your self-esteem. You might need to assess how you feel about your self-esteem if you feel uncomfortable hearing someone say something positive about you. Be proud of yourself and show respect for others. Find people to support and inspire you as you work towards your goals.

2. Keep your eyes on the other person. Pay attention to how your response affects the person you are being kind. Let them know that you appreciate their compliments. Your opinions are important to you.

3. Send us your feelings. Discuss how compliments enhance your day. Perhaps you were nervous about giving your presentation but are now more confident. One perceptive person at least pointed out how intelligent and funny you were.

4. Relax your body. There may be automatic physical reactions you have that cause you to feel uncomfortable when receiving compliments. Instead of looking away, smile and make eye contact. You will instantly feel happier and more connected.

Giving and receiving compliments can brighten your day, no matter how small or large. You can help one another to grow by learning how to express our appreciation.

Why it is important to be selfless sometimes

Do you think being a little selfish can make your life better?

Since childhood, everyone was taught to give back. Consideration for others was a common theme through childhood. Does that mean you should be selfish all the time? It is possible to be selfish from time to time, which can be beneficial for you and your family. There are many reasons selfishness can have a positive impact on your life.

Everyone around you can benefit from you achieving what you desire.

You can be selfish and reap the rewards

1. You will have more joy. Studies have shown that you will feel more joy if you are a little selfish. Happier people are more productive and compassionate. They also tend to be more resilient.

* It's good for your friends, family, coworkers and neighbors. Ask them.

2. You will be healthier. A better quality of life will be possible if you take the time for exercise, sleep well and eat healthy. If you are healthy, you will be better equipped to care for others. You'll also live longer.

3. It's easier than ever to create boundaries and build healthier relationships. While it might seem selfish to ensure your relationships meet your emotional needs fully, it's actually healthy. Other people will find it harder to manipulate you or take

advantage. Any relationship needs to have the ability to say "no".

4. A little self-development can come from being selfish. It's possible to be your best self when you take the time to devote to personal growth. Development takes time and attention. You can't grow if you're selfish.

5. Your life will become more meaningful. Selfishness allows you to surround yourself with the people and things that are most important to you. You must be focused on your own needs to create such a life. What is the best way to accomplish a large goal without being selfish? It is necessary to let go of other distractions in order to accomplish something important.

6. Your attractiveness will be greater to others. Take a look at the person who is least selfish. Do they respect others? Are they full-of-energy and have some control over their lives? Over-altruism can often

lead to exhaustion and run-up of your resources.

* People are drawn to those who dictate their lives. Attractive are success and confidence. Who doesn't admire someone who is confident, happy, and does their best every day? These qualities are impossible to achieve and maintain if you keep your eyes on everyone else.

7. You will be less in need. You'll feel less dependent on others when you're not looking after your own needs. Being dependent on others leads to being dependent upon the wishes of others.

None of these statements are meant to be a endorsement of selfishness. If you go too far, self-centeredness will cause more harm than good. You won't want time with the most selfish person in your life.

A little bit of selfishness can help you have more fun and make it easier to be there for those around you. If you help yourself, others can benefit.

Try to find the balance between focusing solely on yourself and focusing entirely on others. Make time to take care of yourself every day. You will benefit others as well from the benefits you get. Everybody will be thankful for your selfishness.

Non-directive Meditation allows you to take charge of your emotions

Nondirective Meditation may be a helpful option for you if you have trouble with memories or strong feelings. According to a recent study, this type of meditation is more effective in connecting with yourself than regular rest and other meditations.

Non-directive meditation encourages daydreaming, as opposed to focusing on an object or breath. You can learn more about the benefits and how to get started.

Nondirective meditation offers many benefits

1. Increase self-awareness Be aware of what's happening in your head. You can learn a lot about yourself and your values by being aware of how your thoughts are formed. Your ability to communicate effectively with others will improve your ability to promote cooperation.

2. Accept yourself. Anxiety is caused by uncertainty. Your darkest feelings are your best indicator that you can deal with them. You can love yourself, with all of your faults and strengths.

3. Stimulate creativity. Your ability to play becomes less important as we age. It can make you more creative to indulge in fantasies. Perhaps you'll find a quicker way to clean the oven. Perhaps you'll be inspired to create poetry and paint landscapes.

4. Learn to understand others. Flexibility is another advantage. It makes it easier to

imagine yourself in someone else's shoes. You will be able to see important problems from multiple perspectives. Once you know why your child fears thunder, it will be easier to comfort them.

5. Get involved in positive changes. You can get a better idea of your future by looking back on your past. Your insight can be used to help you adopt new habits to get closer to your dreams. Improve your communication skills, or get regular exercise.

How to practice Nondirective Meditation

1. Always be prepared. A healthy body is essential for a healthy mind. Good nutrition and good sleep are key to meditation.

2. Get into position. Relax on a couch or chair. Any position is fine.

3. Let go. Be free to think. Don't be afraid to express your feelings and explore all topics.

4. Forge a resolution. End your session by assigning yourself a task. Talk to your sister or a friend if you are still struggling with not having a prom date. Imagine how much better you'll feel if you can forget about your past.

Nondirective Meditation - Where to Apply

1. You can strengthen your relationships. Interactions with others is where some of our most intense emotions are expressed. Nondirective meditation could help you think differently about a boyfriend or neighbor who is irritating you.

2. You can make your work more meaningful. Imagine your ideal job. This vision could inspire you in your search for a job change or a new role. Consider taking on a new challenge at work or finding a mentor within your field that can help you push beyond your comfort zone.

3. Stay true to your diet. Overeating can cause both happiness and sadness. It is

easier to limit your intake to just one slice of pie if you can control your emotions. Instead of being guided by your emotions, it will be easier to eat only when you are hungry.

4. Your spirituality will be enhanced. Non-directive mediation is an opportunity to explore your life and potential. You will be able clarify what is important to your heart. As you develop your faith, you will be more able to handle hardships and adversity.

Non-directive meditation is a way to achieve more serenity. Let your thoughts take the lead and you can find your true feelings.

Tools to stop panic attacks and stress

People who are "too nice," are often under great stress.

Sometimes being a peacekeeper, or a people pleaser may seem like the best option. However, when you make the decisions necessary to live the lifestyle you desire, you will have to take the initiative and get results. You might feel a little bit stressed.

These ideas will help you to cope with stressful situations and manage panic attacks.

Understanding and managing panic attacks

Panic attacks are common but can be quite frightening. The good news is that you can treat the discomfort with the right treatment. Find out how to manage panic attacks.

Facts About Panic Attacks

1. Be aware of the signs. Panic attacks affect both your mind and your body. You will feel fearful and outof control. Your heart rate starts to rise and you have trouble breathing. You feel shaken and sweaty. Also common are chills, nausea, and hot flashes.

2. Examine the causes. Although the exact cause is still being investigated by

researchers, there are some theories. An increased risk of panic attacks is your family history, substance abuse, and other factors. Personal triggers can lead to panic attacks. You might feel tension suddenly that isn't related to external events.

3. You can let go of all your preconceived notions. You can handle panic attacks by clearing up two myths. Even though panic attacks can make you think you have a heart attack and other serious problems, your body is not at risk. You can still make rational decisions even when you feel stressed.

4. Find out the recovery rates. There are many highly effective treatments. You may find the answers you seek in books, online courses, or consulting a professional. According to some estimates the success rate of treatment is 90%.

How to manage panic attacks

1. Talk with your doctor. Your doctor is a great place to start. They will examine you and recommend treatment.

2. Try medication. As you try to make lifestyle changes, consider medication. Your doctor may recommend antidepressants and anxiety drugs.

3. Talk to a therapist. Many types of therapy are available. Cognitive behavior therapy helps you to develop new ways for thinking and acting. You will learn to identify stress triggers so you can respond more constructively.

4. Breathe deeply. Skilled breathing can help ease any stress. Try taking deep breaths, starting in your abdomen and moving upwards into your chest. As much as possible, exhale as often as you inhale.

5. Accept discomfort. Ironically, we tend to make things worse by trying to avoid difficult situations. In this way we lose the opportunity for our strengths to shine

through and learn valuable lessons. Begin by taking small steps to change the cycle.

6. Wait 10 minutes. Panic attacks may seem like they are eternal, but they only last around 10 minutes. Be assured that it will end soon.

7. Take control of what you are eating. Your diet is a key factor in your well-being. Your body will be more relaxed if you eat healthy whole foods that stabilize your blood sugar. Alcohol and caffeine can increase anxiety.

8. Exercise regularly. Regular exercise is one of your best options for panic attacks. Join a yoga class, or go for an early morning run in your neighborhood park.

9. Support is available. Friends and family might not understand panic attacks or your needs. Find a support group for panic attacks or start your own. It may help you heal faster by sharing your experience with others.

Talk to your doctor about which treatment options might be best for you. It is possible to overcome panic attacks and get back to the things that you love.

Begin Something New: Open to Opportunities

A key aspect of self-development involves the ability and willingness to grab every opportunity that comes your way. You might be wondering about all the possibilities you have. It's great to know your life is filled with hidden treasures that are waiting to be discovered.

These methods can help you to be open to new opportunities.

1. Recognize the many opportunities available to you. Believe that the opportunities you have in your current relationships with people, places, or situations may lead to something greater.

* You can't see the opportunities around your eyes if you are prone to "limiting thinking". Expanding your thinking will help you to see new things.

1. Be open to meeting new people. Meet new people whenever you can. It's helpful to have someone you can network with, or a friend to form a friendship. These associations can help you see opportunities you had not considered.

* Your new colleague might know of a brother that owns a company you could reach out to. You might be interested in running if a new neighbor runs marathons.

1. Eliminate limiting thinking. It is easy to fall into a limiting mindset.

* You could lose your passion, your career, or your monetary wealth if you limit what you think.

* Decide to stop limiting thoughts. You may be just a step away from the next best thing.

1. Avoid running from difficult work projects. You might think "I don't want to participate in this project." But those who are willing to do so learn a lot and have greater future prospects.

* You can make a name for yourself as the "go-to" person and grow your career.

1. Volunteers can fill in for others. You might have a task at work that is not being done. Maybe they feel the task is tedious or boring.

* You might not want to write job descriptions in your department. While everyone may think it's useless, your boss wants it completed. Take charge and get it done.

* Another example could be that your local neighborhood wants to transform a piece land into a small, green park but nobody is willing to help. Get involved and contact your local city council to begin the project.

* You can fill in the gaps and others will notice. This helps you to develop new skills. You can even use some of these jobs as a resume builder.

Your life contains an unknown brilliance you may not have discovered yet. These strategies are your chance to put them into action. Always be open and ready to see and take advantage of any opportunity presented to. A life of abundance awaits you!

Want more? Don't forget to pick up your free 5-day life-altering course, designed to help you attract anything you want, at QueenBeeing.com: http://queenbeeing.com/free-5-day-life-altering-course-attract-anything-want/.

Bonus Section: How you can boost your personal power in just 7 days

This section will provide a seven-day program to help you assert your personal power, and stop placing other people's needs above your own. Take some time to reflect on the affirmations each day. Then, say the affirmations aloud to yourself or in your own mind. Next, meditate on the questions and then journal about them.

Your personal power will increase after the seven-day program. If you still need an extra boost, feel free to continue the program!

Day 1: Wisdom is a better tool than emotion to make decisions.

My experiences in life help me to develop wisdom. The knowledge I have gained from previous situations has helped me make sound judgments.

Emotions are not a factor in my decisions. It is possible for the outcome to be unfavorable if I base my decisions on emotion. When it comes to weighing in on important topics, my head is always steady.

Even though some of the outcomes from my experiences are not what I expected, they have taught me a lot. It helps me to make better choices for the future.

When I'm involved with group decision-making, the team is encouraged to discuss the options. Group discussions encourage sharing of experience and other views.

Anxiety can flare up when there are family issues. Uncontrollable emotions can cause hurtful words, and even actions. I enjoy mediating family matters to help with control of what is said and done. Wisdom allows me to control my feelings.

I feel happier when I make well-thought decisions. This helps me to not live in constant negative emotions. It is important that I have peace of thought.

Today, I want to continue to learn from the world. As I acquire more wisdom, I vow to use it to help other people. I also promise to control my emotions.

Self-Reflection Question: Take some time to reflect on the following questions.

1. How can I discern between a wise and a foolish decision?

2. Is it necessary to feel emotions in order to make a decision?

3. How do I get back on track after allowing my emotions to take over?

Day 2 - Good things happen because I live with positive anticipation

Positive thinking produces positive experiences. There is a direct relationship between my expectations of others and what I experience. I am encouraged and encouraged to think positively.

Positive expectation means that I know my hard work and effort will reap great rewards.

I try to be positive about the people I work with. I am a positive person who shows respect for others. This approach promotes mutual respect and healthy relationships.

Healthy relationships mean successful collaboration. I share my faith in my coworkers. This encourages them and leads to impressive projects.

I get overwhelmed from time to time, but I don't let that stop me from trying to control my emotions. I remind myself that I am blessed.

I know that expecting blessings leads to them being in great proportions. My time is spent on things I can change so that everything else will unfold as planned.

I encourage my friends and family to not worry about what the future holds. My outlook is to believe that there's a solution to every problem in life.

Today I am living proof that positive thinking leads to great things. I pledge to maintain an optimistic outlook. I realize that even if things don't go my way, there are still significant blessings.

Self-Reflection Questions:

1. What positive affirmations could I make each day?

2. How do you respond to a challenge when you expect a positive outcome?

3. Which ways can you share your experiences with others so they feel encouraged to think positively

Day 3 - I am growing in wisdom, strength and courage each day.

Every day is a learning experience. I trust my intuition to direct me to positive options. I can leave behind harmful choices.

I put the knowledge and experience I've gained every day to good use. I learn from my mistakes and from those around me. I have the courage and strength to admit that

I am wrong, and to change my mind if I get on the wrong track.

I am sound in my judgment and have a clear mind. I am brave. I have faith in my ability and capacity to make smart decisions. I know I can choose a positive path for my life.

I am free from the past mistakes. I learn from my mistakes, and I grow wiser every day.

I have a curious spirit. I am aware of people and the events around me. Although I am kind and patient with others I do not allow myself to be easily influenced or misled.

I am wise enough not to forget that I still have much to learn about others and the universe. I am strong enough for the wisdom that my experiences in life can give me.

Today I give thanks to my wisdom and strength. As I continue to grow, I'm grateful for the courage and wisdom that I gain each day.

Self-Reflection Questions:

1. What have my mistakes taught me?

2. What steps should I take in order to gain knowledge and build my strength?

3. Who will mentor me as I seek to become wiser

Day 4 - I get rid the root of all negative attitudes.

My daily goal is to be positive. I know that having a positive and constructive outlook can help me achieve great things. I find the root cause and try to eradicate it.

Negative thinking does not always stand alone, as I have learned. A pessimistic attitude is one that is affected by situations or relationships that are also bad.

How I think about my friends and how they treat me has a huge impact on how I feel. I notice when I'm pondering issues in an unhealthy manner and stop to consider the influence. It can sometimes be hard to decide to leave situations that make me feel low instead of uplifting me. But overall wellness is important.

I decide to end a relationship or environment that is having a negative affect on my health. I take the losses and embrace newfound positivity and my overall health.

To be successful, I need to make my environment supportive. These traits allow me to succeed at every thing I do.

It is very beneficial to have a positive mindset. It attracts positive thinkers, who also focus on building instead of breaking. It makes me feel happier.

I still work to remove any negative aspects from my daily life. My family, friends, work, and colleagues are all there to lift me up. I will open myself up to positive situations to allow me to have uplifting moments.

Self-Reflection Questions:

1. What techniques are there to help me gently break up with unhealthy relationships?

2. Which ways can I make a difference in creating a hostile environment?

3. How can I make a difference in creating a positive working environment?

Day 5: My happiness is mine.

I take a bold step in the direction of my dreams, goals, hopes and dreams, leaving behind my past. Each step I take brings me closer toward a happier, better me.

I am the one who decides my fate, no matter what happens in the past. I have the ability to create my own path and reach my highest dreams.

When I take control of my life, I am content.

Each day brings us more joy. I can find goodness in all things, regardless of their circumstances.

I am open to exploring new places and experiencing new experiences as I move forward on my journey. I have everything I need for a happy, fulfilling life. This gives me hope and confidence.

I'm able to quickly find a way around obstacles so I can continue my journey. These obstacles are fun and help me stay focused on the things that matter to me.

Today, I am happy because of how I treat myself. I make an effort to take the time every day to unwind and recharge. I choose to be happy and bring joy.

Self-Reflection Questions:

1. What are some activities that bring you joy in your daily life?

2. What are my deepest needs?

3. What tasks can be delegated so I have time to do the things that I love most

Day 6 - I am grateful for small successes that lead me to greater goals.

Small successes are small victories that I am grateful for. I know that small steps lead to significant goals.

I accept the challenges that I know I can conquer. I do not try to overcome the enormity of a huge end result. Instead, I try to focus on achievable goals and celebrate the small victories.

Sometimes, it seems like debt is an ever-present challenge. I feel discouraged when I see my total debt. Sometimes, I feel as though I don't have enough resources to pay my debts.

I do give myself credit for the small, steady payments I am capable of making each month. I set reasonable repayment goals and feel encouraged to make them.

My career plans are moving nicely because I am focused solely on the current journey. I am not concerned about how far I need to go. I strive to achieve today's goals.

Today, small successes are a big part of how proud I feel about my achievements. Knowing that small successes are a sign of my potential to reach bigger goals, I believe it is an indicator of my capability to do so. I vow to persevere on the road towards greatness.

Self-Reflection Questions:

1. What have I learned from my success?

2. Why is it important to acknowledge even the smallest achievements?

3. How do small goals help me in other areas?

Day 7: Everyday I become stronger in my mind, body, soul, and spirit.

Every day holds the potential to make you stronger. These opportunities present themselves to me. Growth is something that interests me.

I always find new ways to strengthen my mind. I challenge my thinking and beliefs. I find that challenge increases my ability to overcome adversity.

My body is treated with respect. I eat healthy food to ensure my body gets the nutrients it needs. For strength and fitness, I work out on a regular basis. I get the sleep that I need to feel alert, well rested, and awake every night.

Prayer and meditation are ways I nourish my soul. I can strengthen my spirituality by giving these activities constant attention.

Small improvements are easy to achieve in each area. It takes very little stress to make small, incremental improvements that produce excellent results. These are small, easy changes that I can make.

Today I am determined to improve every aspect of who I am. I view every challenge as an opportunity to grow. My mind is growing stronger, as well as my body and soul.

Self-Reflection Questions:

1. What can I do right now to challenge my mind? To increase my ability to deal with adversity

2. What changes can you make to your diet to boost your health?

3. How can I include prayer and meditation in my life?

What causes people to be petty?

Let's dive into the main content of this chapter now that we have explored all the possible forms of people-pleasing. As we know (and as you likely already know if your book was picked up), people-pleasing has a draining effect. We have to ask ourselves why people do it. Why do you do it? That's the next topic we will discuss.

- From parent pleasers, to people-pleasers

People-pleasers usually start out as parents pleasers. This characteristic (people-pleasing), can be inherited from your childhood when you try to maintain closeness and connection with parents who are often unavailable. This can lead to the formation of what psychologists Mary Ainsworth, John Bowlby, and Mary Ainsworth call the anxious attachment type.

People-pleasers parents tend to be more concerned with themselves and their lives that their children. They may misunderstand their child's behavior and emotions, or they can become emotionally overwhelmed. They may be unable to respond to their child's needs, or they might not do it consistently. Inborn instincts tell children to seek out connection with their parents. When this is not achieved, they learn to do all they can to satisfy that need. They are likely to seek out their parents' attention and cling to them. In some cases, the roles might be reversed and the children may assume the parental role of caring for their parents. "Mum feels tired. I should make mum breakfast. "I should clean up her house. She looks tired." You should be aware that this is not just being a good kid.

Research has also shown that children's attachment styles can influence their parents' parenting practices. If you grew up in an unhappy home with a parent who was not available, you are likely to develop a similar attachment type.

The child does exactly what the parents ask. Achieves the goals and dreams set by their parents. High achiever, perfectionist. They aren't interested in learning who they are.

It can be said that people-pleasing is partially caused by the emotional inconsistency between parents. Children do whatever they can to earn the love of their parents. Children who developed an anxious attachment style in childhood internalize the belief that they have to go above and beyond for the love of others.

- Past Trauma

Sometimes people-pleasers will act in a way that is triggered by trauma. A few people who have been physically or emotionally abused may find it safer to do what they are told to do. For them, it's safer to take care others' needs first than to tend to their own. This can help avoid any trouble. This occurs subconsciously.

Issues related to self-esteem

It might be difficult to forget the memories of your past relationships. Some people have been in relationships with others who were cruel or down-on. It is not easy to let go traumatic memories from past relationships.

They also have negative beliefs about themselves and they carry these beliefs from relationship to relationship. If you were to learn that others could judge your value, you will likely go to great lengths for others to prove it. If you don't address this belief, it will follow you wherever and whenever you go.

Chapter 5: People-Pleasing At A Cost

The price of people-pleasing is definitely high. It takes away some things which we have already discussed in the previous chapter. You can be a people pleaser, which can make it hard for you to love yourself. There are many negative experiences that can occur, some of which will be explored below.

People-pleasing doesn't seem to be inherently wrong. It involves empathy, compassion, and altruism. These are usually desirable traits. They are generally derived from a place where there is love. This is where the problem lies. You put so much effort into earning this love that it is difficult to take care of your own needs. It's acting. People will love you if you do the same things. They will expect you to say the things they want. You are dressing how you think they want you. Your actions are a reflection of your inauthenticity, with yourself as well as with others. Here are some costs to being a people-pleaser.

- People will be able to take advantage of your abilities

It is not difficult for someone to be eager to please. The cheerleaders are already aware that this girl is willing to kiss them. Your boss knows you'd work extra hours for him if he asked. You may not have been told by your boss that you are a people-pleaser. But they know that they can trust you to do what they ask. They realize that you are always available for them and so they make the most of it. They will keep asking you questions, and you'll keep saying yes. They will keep asking for more and more until you set boundaries. We will be discussing boundaries more in chapter 3.

- You will feel resentful.

People will appreciate you doing the right thing for them. They are able to see what you do and how you sacrifice for them.

Resentment creeps in when you realise they are taking advantage. Because the habit is so deeply embedded in subconscious beliefs, we have seen it continue doing it. It's a way of life that you can't escape. This leads you to frustration. This can lead to frustration. You could become passive-aggressive, which will harm you and the people that you're trying so hard to please.

- Your relationships won't satisfy you

Relationships revolve around giving and receiving. It's about giving and receiving. You give each other gifts, do things for one-another, help one another out, listen to each other and are there for one an another. That's how a healthy partnership works. It's easy to become a draining relationship if the relationship is a one-way one, where you are the only giver. People-pleasers can often find themselves in such situations.

Only if you do things for people who are like you, will you feel fulfilled and happy in a relationship. People-pleasing is not acting. You're not the other person in the relationship. You are simply trying to make other people happy, whether you know it or not. This becomes increasingly difficult as you age. It makes you tired, and you don't feel satisfied in your relationship, even though you're doing the right thing.

You will feel exhausted and stressed.

This is probably the most obvious cost of people-pleasing. If you continue to take on more than your abilities, burnout is inevitable. You will soon find yourself lacking the time and energy to enjoy your hobbies and interests. You'll eventually suffer the physical and mental consequences if you work late or run errands.

People around you will start to notice your people-pleasing lifestyle.

Your spouse will notice that your work hours are longer.

Your friends will notice that your yes to everything is a sign of respect.

Your parents will notice you keep apologizing to your parents even if you are not wrong.

It will stress and strain you.

What is the best thing about being a people-pleaser! People will begin to rely on you when you show that you are willing and able to do any task they ask.

Your coworkers know that you're coming to work for coffee.

Your house will always remain open for those parties, cheerleaders can tell.

Your classmates will be able to see that you have done their homework.

These people will no longer do these tasks for themselves, but will depend entirely on you. I don't know what this makes you feel, but it is stressful.

- You will soon lose your self

The deep sea of people-pleasing can make you forget who your true self is. People-pleasers excel at playing the part of whoever they are at any given time. It is easy to forget who you are. What do your interests actually entail? What are you really passionate about? It is possible to lose the things that you love and used to enjoy before everyone else dictated them. It's like you forget who you really were to become someone others would like.

The cheerleaders will like the girl who is envious of her. She will also join them in making fun of her friends. She might not like it but she does it anyway. Isn't this her losing herself? A significant loss is to lose touch and feel connected with oneself. You will lose your creativity and drive. The mirror is all you see of yourself. Instead, you only see the person that you are meant to be.

Low self-esteem will result

People-pleasers are often highly self-critical. You will never feel complete. To feel accepted and loved, you attempt to be someone other than yourself. Insecurity makes you seek out validation. What happens if you don't get the validation you need? You will become even more critical about yourself.

- You'll be alone

Beyonce sings, "I don't feel at home in the home I call home." This is what people-pleasers feel most of all the time. This feeling is similar to being trapped in someone else's body or disassociated from your true self. You can be with people but feel lonely. Why is this so? It is because you are acting. It's like wearing a mask. This high school girl may be enjoying cheerleaders and is not content. Even though you're now part of the conversation, your colleagues still don't feel like they are there for you. It is because you are not your true self. The attention you seek to be is there, but you're not the one you are trying to be.

Imagine them calling your "Coffee Guy", but include you in their conversations. Are you going to feel truly connected? No. They do not know you. They just know who you are. Every day, they know who the person is who brings them coffee. This feeling of loneliness is not going away, even if they are receiving the attention they so desperately desire.

It can be extremely frustrating to be there, but not fully present. You want love, to be loved, and to be needed. It is why you do what you do. You long for companionship. Intimacy, happiness, and a sense that you are part of something bigger. But you feel lonely. People don't push you away. You talk with them and have fun, but something is missing. Role-playing, and keeping yourself back from others can lead to isolation.

- You will feel powerless.

Doing what others expect you to do shows you care, are polite and considerate. You'll feel powerless. This is how it works. If you do these things, it is normal to expect things to go well and people will reciprocate. Sometimes things don't go as planned. You feel as though you don't have enough power or influence to make an impact on others.

Some people grow, meet love, and are promoted. But you stay the same, trying not to break the rules. It will make you feel guilty. You tell yourself you are not as selfish as the other people. You tell your self that you are a decent person. And then, life becomes easy for you. Things seem too difficult to manage so you give up. They seem too daunting and hard to attain or you are wrong. You may doubt your ability or capability to achieve anything.

- You'll lose your freedom

A people-pleaser can be described as a child. A little child that will only do what is asked. A people-pleaser can't be rebellious, even the smallest of things. A people-pleaser can't say no. They would trade their freedom for the chance to be liked or fit in. So how are they going to ever feel free? How can they make their own decisions? People-pleasers can feel trapped. The funny thing is, they have their own cage.

- You will get over-thinking and become unnecessarily nervous

What if they don't love me? What if they think I am crazy? Why is there so many comments on my picture? Would I have been better off if that happened? This is how the brain works of people-pleasers. They worry too often. They don't want anyone to be upset. They don't like to say the wrong things. It's a recipe for anxiety. You create an environment where you can't hurt anyone and then you make it worse. The same applies to when you try to do too much and you end up sacrificing your own personal needs.

Chapter 6: Boundaries, How To Define, Communicate, And Maintain Them

This chapter and the following three will be about ways you can stop being a people-pleaser. As we've seen, people-pleasers struggle to establish boundaries. This chapter will talk about boundaries and how they can be defined, communicated, and maintained.

Not being able to set boundaries for yourself is a good thing. This doesn't mean you have to shut down people or push them away. It is simply a way to get to know yourself better and ensure your needs are being met.

How can you draw boundaries and limit your options? How do you decide what people can and can't say or do to your face? How do you determine what you can and cannot tolerate? These are the questions that you will find answers to.

- When you interact and communicate with others, be honest about your feelings

Emotions are messengers. They can help us understand what is important in any situation. The first and most important step in setting boundaries is to recognize your needs. It's crucial to be aware of how other people feel. There are many emotions that can be experienced, such as anger or frustration, anxiety or overwhelm. When you observe how each person makes it feel, you'll be able to determine where, when, how and with whom boundaries should be set. Take note of your feelings when you're around colleagues. Do you feel like you're being used? Are you happy to get their cups of coffee? When you recognize how you feel about certain activities and people, you can set boundaries. These feelings are not to be ignored. Ask yourself why you feel the way you do. This exercise may seem challenging at first. Like all skills, it is learned by practicing. You will develop a greater awareness of your emotions with time. This will enable you to better understand your needs.

- Talk about what boundaries you are setting

People around you must know your limits and boundaries. They will keep asking you to get coffee, even if they don't know that you don't prefer to be sent to coffee. Until she informs them, the cheerleaders would assume that the girl's place is available for their parties. However, it's not a good idea to start a dispute or fight. Simply share with them your determination to set boundaries. Explain to them why this is important and what it will do for you. Giving yourself time to yourself is beneficial, and if you care deeply about others, they will also understand.

- Accept it when other people establish boundaries

People who have trouble setting boundaries often have difficulty accepting others' boundaries. You want others to respect your boundaries. When people tell you about their boundaries, express your gratitude. Be sincere and say "I appreciate the honesty"

Learn how you can say no to someone without explaining your reasons

Sometimes it's not necessary to explain who you are. It is acceptable to say no when asked to do something that you do not want. Not giving an excuse or a reason can make you feel guilty, especially when you have to justify it. Try to say "no" instead of giving an excuse. If a friend invites you to the movies and you refuse to go, say "no", because you don't feel like going tonight. One simple no is enough to ensure that nobody gets hurt. You can master this skill over time. Don't get discouraged if you find it difficult to remain firm at first. In Chapter 6, we'll explore additional ways to say "no".

- Make a list indicating who must be aware of your boundaries and who does not.

Not everyone needs to be aware of all your boundaries. The real question is: Who needs to know and what doesn't? This is where your VIP List comes in. While it might not be an actual list of people, this will allow you to decide who needs explanations as to why your boundaries are set. This is because it's not a good idea to share too much personal information with people you don't really need. If you share too much with people that aren't your closest or don't care about what you're going through, it can make you feel uncomfortable and uneasy.

Create a list of the things you want to share with everyone, and the ones you prefer to keep to yourself. This will help you feel secure and create a trusting community.

- Break from any unhealthy relationship or friendship

You need to be able to recharge and take good care of yourself. That might not be possible if there are toxic people around. Don't give your friend the power to take more than you give. You can't depend upon your friends for everything so give them space. If friends don't return favors, allow them to be friends. Setting boundaries means letting go of relationships and friendships that suffocate. This is one of most challenging aspects of boundary-setting, yet it is also one of most rewarding. Break up with any relationship that makes your feel disregarded, unheard, and unseen. You are not selfish. You care about your well being.

- Keep in mind that your boundaries will change a lot after you set them.

It might be difficult to adjust your boundaries. It's normal to feel self-conscious, guilty, and embarrassed after setting boundaries. Remind yourself of why you have set boundaries and why they are important to be maintained. Keep in mind the cost of people-pleasing as we have discussed in the last chapter. Imagine what it could bring you if these consequences were not in your life.

- Get someone to guide you through your journey

When working towards a goal, it is extremely important to have someone who will support you and hold you responsible. It could be your parent, a friend, a partner or anyone you trust. Share your successes with someone. Someone who will motivate you when your self-criticism or inability to keep up. This person will be your confidant, cheerleader. They will learn about your goals, why you set them and what it means to you. They will then meet with you to check in on you and offer support as you travel. Both of them would celebrate small victories, and then look for ways to improve.

Imagine how different your daily life would look if you created new boundaries

You can imagine how different your life would look if you had your boundaries in place. Imagine how different your life would be if your boundaries were in place. It is possible to stand up for yourself and not allow others to exploit you. Imagine how happy and liberated you'd be, and how much you could spend on the things that you love.

Establishing healthy boundaries is essential in dealing with people-pleasing behaviors. Before you say yes to a request for a favour from someone, think about these:

Is this something you would like to do or not?

What will make me feel happy?

What happens when I must sacrifice time that I have set aside for another purpose?

If you agree with your answers to these questions then please help. If you aren't comfortable answering the questions, you can just say, "No. Thanks." Or you could say "No, this won't work". Be sure you ask before you give up on someone. It is not your obligation to please anyone.

What's next after setting boundaries?

Setting boundaries does not mean you will become cruel or cease to be kind. This does not mean that you should disregard others and lose interest in them. It means that you decide what makes your happy and what does not. There is a fine line between what you can handle and what your limits are. It's about saying "yes," to others but not to yourself.

Even if you do not set boundaries, you can still be helpful. You can still show kindness if your heart is in it. Make sure you always consider yourself first. If you don't care enough about yourself, it will be difficult to take care of others. Sometimes, it is best to give others the best of yourself. You must first take care of your own needs before you can help someone else.

One last note. When you set boundaries, be sure to stick to them. It may feel uncomfortable at the beginning and it will take some effort. There is a possibility that you will fall back to old habits from now on. It's normal for self-development to have moments when you fall back on old habits. This skill is just like any other. It becomes easier to practice. It is important to remember why you set your boundaries and what the benefits are. Then you will have to decide between staying put and accepting the pain associated with creating a life that is more fulfilling for you.

Chapter 7: Ask What You Want

People-pleasers often have trouble asking for what they desire. They won't ask for what you want, as they don't want to be inconvenienced. Strangely, they are always willing to allow others inconvenience them. People-pleasers are unable to see that in order to make others happy, one must first be happy. To satisfy others, one must first satisfy himself.

Let's look at pleasing oneself. If you are a people pleaser, you will find that other people treat you differently than you treat them. It can hurt. This can be changed by changing your perceptions. If you can change your thinking, you will see a shift in your behaviour. Here are some points to be aware of:

You don't love or respect your self when you cause pain to others.

- When you agree to do something you do not want, you are not loving and respecting yourself.

- When people disregard your boundaries without consequence, you're not loving and respecting yourself.

- If you look at others' dissatisfaction, you don't love or respect yourself.

You don't love or respect yourself when you do the same things as others.

Why are people afraid to ask for what is best for them?

Most people won't ask for things they don't want out of pride. Some people think asking is a sign of weakness or incompetence. They want to be able to solve everything on their own. But it's quite different when it involves people-pleasers. Here are some reasons they won't ask for what you want.

- Low self-esteem

People-pleasers will not ask for things they do not deserve. A people-pleaser may not ask to be given a raise as they believe they do not deserve it. Because the girl doesn't feel they will listen to her anyway, she wouldn't tell the cheerleaders she couldn't have her house used for parties anymore. Or she believes or knows she can easily be disposed of. They are the only thing that holds them together.

- Not having any goals

You can take a moment and ask yourself what it is that you really want. Do you have a clear vision of your life? Have you got a vision of what your life should look like? Many people don't know exactly what they want. When they are given the chance to request what they want, many people don't know where to start. That's a terrible situation! Unable to know how to ask for what it is you want could be another challenge. Although you know exactly what you want, and where you want it from.

However, how do they ask? How do you ask your boss for an increase? How do cheerleaders stop bringing their friends over to your house? How can you make your spouse respect you

Fear

People avoid asking for what it is they are afraid of. Fear of rejection, ridicule and being laughed at are some of the reasons you might be afraid to ask for what you want. You fear your boss will laugh at you when you ask for raises. In fact, they might call their secretary to tell the boss how funny you were. If you tell your spouse that you don't agree with their treatment of you, they might get in a fight. Fear doesn't make you go anywhere. Fear holds you back. It's better not to ask for the raise but get mocked, than to keep trying to please your boss every day without getting proper compensation. It's better not to suffer poor treatment than to openly tell your spouse what you think.

How to Get What You Want

Ask someone you trust to share it with you

You're not going tell your neighbour that cheerleaders should stop coming over. If you want them stop coming, let them know. You must know who can give what you want. Let me illustrate. Let's say that a woman complains about her husband every day to the hairdresser. She does it every time but never tells him. She has never spoken out against him. Do you think he will ever learn to be more responsible? You're wrong. This is why I suggest asking for someone who can help you. Ask the person who you want to know what it is and be open about it.

Ask with confidence

You don't have to ask for something confidently. It's a sign that you are confident about your request and believe you have earned the item. You can project confidence through your body language. Your body language can convey confidence. This includes standing straight, making eye contact and using confident words. It's important to ask for something as if your expectation is that you will receive it. Trust me, confidence does make a difference.

Ask Clearly

You have the courage to ask what you want. Don't be afraid to ask. Don't be a shaming machine. Don't be afraid to state clearly what you want. Don't be shy about stating your wishes. Be as specific as possible. The more detailed you are, the easier it will be for your request to be granted. Tell your spouse exactly what they like and don't. Tell your boss how big a raise you are looking for. Please be specific.

- Make a strategy

Human beings tend to be selfish. People will not do any good if there is no gain for them. If you're asking someone for something, let them know what they would gain if they granted your request. Tell your boss that you understand your worth and that the salary you receive isn't fair. You can tell your boss all the positive things that you do for your company and what extra value it could offer if you get the right opportunity and compensation. Seek out evidence of the positive contributions you have made to the organization. It is possible to have letters and reports from colleagues that prove how much you are deserving of the raise. It's not necessary to make it personal. Be confident.

Ask consistently

"No" does NOT mean never. If you request for the first-time, and it is denied, take some time to reconsider your request and ask again. Don't be afraid to deal with resistance. It is important to be creative in the way that you present your request. It is not a good idea to keep repeating the exact same thing over and again. Try to find other ways of expressing it. If you aren't sure who to ask, find the right person. Find the right moment for you to ask. Keep trying. Remember that "no" could be used to mean "not yet", "not here", or "not right now", but not necessarily "never."

How do you get rid of the fear of asking what you want?

We've already stated that fear is one reason people don't want what they want. So, how do they overcome their fear? It's okay to be scared. Fear should not overwhelm you. First, you need to understand why you are so afraid. One example is if you want to request a raise but are afraid that your boss won't approve or will get mad at. Although none of this has happened yet, it's still a stressful situation. Acknowledge the fact that you're the one who created this fear. It might help you to get over it.

You can also overcome your fear of asking someone for what they want by realizing that you won't ever get it if you ask. If you do not ask, it will always return a "no".

When you finally ask, and get a no, what are you doing? That's right. You don't have much to lose.

Chapter 8: Quit Chasing Approval

In this chapter, I will be reminding you that what you think of yourself is more important then what anyone else thinks about you. It's just like you can't imagine anyone loving you if your heart isn't full of love. Your opinion of yourself is more important that any other person's. This chapter is about quitting looking for approval.

What does it really mean to chase approval The goal of chasing approval is to find external validation. It is the use of external validation as a measure for self-worth. Fear of taking on new tasks or doing new things is a sign that you don't want to be judged or make others think less of yourself. To seek approval means to try hard to be perfect so you don't get ridiculed. A people-pleaser will avoid conflict wherever possible. A people-pleaser will seek approval to feel happy, accept accomplishments, be available for productivity, and enjoy admiration.

How to Quit Looking For Approval

- Increase your self awareness

Doing this requires that you be gentle with yourself. After years of being people-pleasers, how can you cease to care about other people's approval? It's not an easy process. Don't let your inner turmoil and anxiety get in the way of your progress. It is important to be gentle with your self as you transition into new behaviors and thoughts.

Your behaviours are the first step to taking control of your life. You should take note of what you say or do to get approval. Next, think about what you would do or speak differently if the person accepted you for who are.

This will allow you to see the possibility in your brain. It will also help you identify when you're being authentic and acting. This is what self-awareness means.

Find out what makes You Happy

This is critical. Why? Because it lets you know when to set boundaries or say no. Notice when you are happy, and when you don't. It's important to be aware of your emotions. Pay attention to when you feel happy. Find the activities that lift you up and make time for them. It could be knitting or reading, listening and dancing to music, talking to friends, walking on the beach with family, or just about anything that makes you happy. Do what makes your heart happy.

- Take some time to think about whether you want to be a helper or a friend.

If someone asks you a question, you don't always have the answer you want right away. Give yourself time to think about the question. The request may require you to take five, twenty, or thirty minutes. This will allow time for you to determine if this is something you enjoy doing and if you have enough resources to complete the task. It is easier to be open with yourself when you are not under pressure. Viktor Frankl, neurologist, stated, "Between stimulation and response, there are two things." There is a space between stimulus and response that allows us to choose the best response. Our freedom and growth are in the response we give. You are giving up your power to other people by saying yes to every request. Give yourself that space. Use that time. Reclaim your power.

Prepare a script of how you would respond to "no" ahead of time.

Some people have difficulty expressing themselves and get stuck. They don't know how or when to say "no", and how to do it without sounding rude. Preparing a script is a solution. Be respectful and firm when writing your script if you don't want anyone to feel hurt. It is important to clearly communicate what you feel, and your boundaries. This can be as simple as "You know I love you, but it's not my day." Or "Thank you for asking, but it's not possible to make it." It's possible to set boundaries, say no, and still be respectful.

Make the right decision for you

After you've achieved self-awareness, discovered your happiness, learned how to say no and practiced taking the time to think before making a decision, you are ready for you to take control of your life.

You can still take your time. Start with people you trust and your family. Tell them "no" when you can and then tell them the truth. There are good chances you will get great results. This will boost your confidence. This is possible because you can choose to speak your truth and not be influenced by other people. Every time you choose the best for yourself, you build self-esteem.

Instead of trying to be validated by others or comparing yourself to them, why not try to define yourself according to your ideal self. Who do you desire to be and why? Identify the person you wish to be, and the qualities they possess. Then, start to cultivate these habits and values. Ask yourself questions like:

- What can you do better?

- What do you believe is right?

- What values should I have?

- What should I believe?

How can I learn more?

Acceptance doesn't necessarily mean respect. If you believe it does you will automatically rely on the popular opinions. You would not be able to defend your position. Refusing to reveal information and refusing to express your opinions is a sign that you're doing more harm then good. You make it impossible for others to correct their wrongs, change behaviours, or make the right decisions.

People-pleasers believe they need to choose between being friendly and being truthful. But, as we've seen, you can hold your ground and still remain respectful. It's okay to say "no" politely. Not all disagreements have to be rude. It is possible to politely decline something.

You have something to say. Don't be afraid to speak up. You can say "no" if you don't want to. You can speak up to let others know what you think and to not conform to their expectations.

This may seem uncomfortable at first. However, you can find strength in knowing that your actions are right. This is the most effective method to communicate.

A confidence folder is one way to boost your self-confidence. It is a list of positive and encouraging emails, praise letters, cards, and letters. You can access this file when you're feeling down or need to get approval from someone. A list of accomplishments or other items that would make your feel worthy can be included in the file.

Why do you need to stop seeking approval from the outside?

There are many reasons why you should not seek validation from people. I'll talk about some of them below.

- Total freedom only comes when we accept who we really are and not pretending to be. What do you want people liking about you? Don't pretend to be someone you aren't.

- It is possible not to be rude or mean and be kind. Kindness doesn't require you to do everything. Being kind means helping people out of love. It is not lying to make people happy, but telling them the truth.

Do what is important to you and you will be happier. People don't make you happier.

Inner peace comes from choosing yourself and what is important for you. It is not about you being selfish. It's your love for yourself.

- Lastly: When you live your life on your terms, doing what makes you happy, your confidence will grow, and you'll be proud of your accomplishments.

Chapter 9: Watch Your Language Choice

We know that people-pleasers struggle to express themselves. These people don't know what to do or how to express themselves. Your feelings do not have to be wrong. What matters is how you express these feelings.

Try to use "I" in your sentences, rather than "you" when expressing yourself. You won't seem to be accusing or blaming someone by doing this. Instead of saying "You treat Me like a 3-year-old", you can say "I feel that You don't Respect Me and Treat me Like a Child".

Also, be specific. This is something I mentioned in chapter 4. Use precise language when asking for something or setting boundaries. Be specific and don't say "You never listens to me," instead talk about a particular time they were not listening to you.

It's important to listen to others when you are expressing your thoughts. It's a conversation. To solve the problem, try to cooperate.

These skills will allow you to be assertive in communicating and expressing yourself at work, home, or wherever else you might find yourself.

What is Assertive Communication, exactly?

In simple words, assertive communication refers to healthy and effective communication. In unhealthy communication, you either remain passive (you don't speak out for yourself) and/or aggressive (you use disrespectful, hurtful expressions or tone of voice). None of these communication types can help you ask for what your want or live a people pleasing-free lifestyle.

Assertiveness can be described as the bridge between the two of you. Assertive communication is calm, respectful communication. It's communication in which both parties listen and speak. We have discussed the use of "I", which is a great method for assertive communication. Keep in mind to use "I", instead of "you," as often as possible.

Passive vs Assertive Behaviour

People-pleasers often exhibit passive behavior. It's when you're too shy and too easygoing. You agree too quickly and too frequently. You may say things such as "I'll enjoy whatever you're having", or "I'll be okay with whatever decision I make", often referring to yourself. When a person acts passively, they feel that their thoughts and feelings don't matter as much as other people's. You are too passive to let others disrespect you or take you as their own.

To be too passive leads to internal conflict. That is, conflict with your self. It can lead you to anger, guilt, feeling victimized, and a need for revenge.

Aggressive vs Assertive Behavior

This is the antithesis of passive. People-pleasers shouldn't be aggressive. This goes against everything people-pleasing stands behind. An aggressive person wants others to think they are better than them. They can be disrespectful and humiliating to others, even threatening them with physical violence.

It isn't the right way to deal with things. You may be able to get what you want at times, but it will not earn respect. It can make people feel intimidated or resentful.

Passive-aggressive vs Assertive Behavior

Passive-aggressive individuals are somewhere between passive and aggressive. This type of person can both say "no" when needed and give their approval when necessary. These people can be a nuisance to others, but not face-to-face. In addition, instead of speaking up, passive-aggressive individuals show what they feel through their actions. Passive-aggressive people don't speak up about their emotions. It is common for passive-aggressive people to cause conflict in relationships.

What stops you from being assertive?

- The absence of practice

It is essential to start small, just as I said before. Start small. Practice setting boundaries with your family and friends. Begin to learn how to express yourself, either at home or with a small group. Once you get comfortable with it, it will feel natural to express yourself.

Fear of rejection

People who have suffered rejection over and over again will know this. They fear rejection. This is why they can't say the things that are on their minds or say "no". Sometimes it's just in their heads, their fears and insecurities telling them that they will be rejected.

- Wanting peace

Some people are afraid to face conflict. They are more comfortable with letting the world go and allowing others to do the same. Yes, people can disagree with you and say hurtful comments if you are openly expressing yourself. These comments can be hurtful if you don't like yourself or feel confident about your abilities. If you are confident in your own worth, others' opinions won't matter as much.

Why is it important for Assertiveness to be Important?

- We'll meet all your needs

It is possible to get what you want when you ask for it clearly. As I have said, people do not possess mind-reading abilities. If you don't ask for it, they won't know what you need. If you ask, they might grant it.

- You will feel understood

Did you recall what we said regarding people-pleasing behavior acting like you act? People won't get to know you, so they won't be able understand you. If you only do people-please, then you're hiding who and what you are. If you are assertive, people can see the real YOU and begin to understand.

- Self-esteem will increase

Being able and confident in your own abilities will make you more confident. Your self-esteem will rise if you are confident.

- Respect will be shown to both parties

Healthy communication will increase the respect of both parties. It shows respect for the person that you're speaking to and earns you respect from other people. You are demonstrating that you are worthy to be respected and that your opinions count.

What are the advantages of being assertive?

The best communication style is assertiveness. It will benefit you to be assertive

Earn respect by earning it

Recognize and Understand Your Feelings

- Increase self-confidence

You can increase your self-esteem

Create strong relationships

Express yourself effectively

- better job satisfaction

It's easier to get what you want from other people

How to become assertive

- Get to know your style

What is your approach to people-pleasing? Do you find yourself saying "yes" to anything, even when you have a lot of work? Are you the type who cannot express what you feel? Are you the kind of person that is easily ridiculed or inflicted by others? To change your style, regardless of what type you are, you need to first get to know it.

- Use "I", statements

Instead of saying "I don't think you are right", say, "I disagree with your opinion." This makes you seem more respectful and opens up the possibility of having a discussion.

- Say "no" often

You may be so enthralled by people who say "yes" all day, that you don't want to change your mind. Try saying "no". You can be firm about this. Simply say, "No. I can't make it right now." If you need to explain, don't be too long. You don't have to explain everything.

- Practice what you want to say

This is true if there's a major or serious confrontation, such as with your boss. Plan it before you go. You can make a list of what you want to communicate and then follow it up with a script. You can think of different scenarios and imagine what you would do if they happened. You can ask a friend, colleague, or coworker to help.

- Use bodylanguage

Confidence is impossible when you're looking at someone's face and not the ground. Be confident even when you don't feel that way. Try to keep eye contact with your friend and have a neutral facial expression. You can practice this with a friend.

www.ingramcontent.com/pod-product-compliance
Lightning Source LLC
Chambersburg PA
CBHW050408120526
44590CB00015B/1873